POEMS I LIKE

Books of poetry by Mary Wilson

Selected Poems
New Poems

POEMS I LIKE

*An anthology chosen
by Mary Wilson*

Hutchinson
London Melbourne Sydney Auckland Johannesburg

Hutchinson & Co. (Publishers) Ltd

An imprint of the Hutchinson Publishing Group

17-21 Conway Street, London W1P 6JD

Hutchinson Group (Australia) Pty Ltd
30-32 Cremorne Street, Richmond South, Victoria 3121
PO Box 151, Broadway, New South Wales 2007

Hutchinson Group (NZ) Ltd
32-34 View Road, PO Box 40-086, Glenfield, Auckland 10

Hutchinson Group (SA) Pty Ltd
PO Box 337, Bergvlei 2012, South Africa

First published 1983

Set in VIP Palatino by
D. P. Media Limited, Hitchin, Hertfordshire

Printed in Great Britain by The Anchor Press Ltd,
and bound by Wm Brendon & Son Ltd,
both of Tiptree, Essex

British Library Cataloguing in Publication Data

Poems I like.
1. English poetry
I. Wilson, Mary
821'.008   PR1174
ISBN 0 09 150650 6

Acknowledgements

Thanks are due to the following for permission to reproduce work in this anthology:

Hutchinson Publishing Group for 'A Bookshop Idyll' by Kingsley Amis

Tony Armstrong for 'For Bryher'

Faber and Faber Ltd for 'O what is that sound?' by W. H. Auden, from *Collected Poems*

John Murray (Publishers) Ltd for 'Station Syren' and 'Sunday Morning, King's Cambridge' by John Betjeman, from *Collected Poems*

The Literary Trustees of Walter de la Mare and The Society of Authors for 'Nod' and 'Fare Well' by Walter de la Mare

Faber and Faber Ltd for 'Journey of the Magi' by T. S. Eliot from *Collected Poems 1909–1962*

The Mitre Press for 'Winter Sunset' and 'Leaf' by Richard Gomm

David Higham Associates Ltd for 'Santa Claus in a department store' by Christopher Hassall, from *Collected Poems*

Adrian Henri for 'Mrs Albion You've Got a Lovely Daughter', Adrian Henri, from *Modern Poets 10*

Hodder and Stoughton Ltd for 'Remembrance Day' by Quintin Hogg, from *The Devil's Own Song and Other Verses*

The Poems of Gerard Manley Hopkins edited by W. H. Gardner and N. H. Mackenzie for 'Spring'

The Society of Authors and Jonathan Cape Ltd for 'Into My Heart' by A. E. Housman

Andre Deutsch Ltd for 'Answers' by Elizabeth Jennings

Macmillan Ltd and the National Trust for 'The Way Through the Woods' by Rudyard Kipling

George Allen and Unwin for 'All Day it has Rained' by Alun Lewis, from *Raiders Dawn*

A. D. Peters and Co. Ltd for 'The Devourers' by Rose Macaulay

MacGibbon and Kee Ltd for 'The Two Parents' by Hugh
    MacDiarmid, from *Collected Poems*
The Society of Authors for 'Twilight' by John Masefield
The Estate of Sir Arthur Quiller-Couch for 'Alma Mater'
    by Arthur Quiller-Couch
George Allen and Unwin for 'Envoi' by Kathleen Raine,
    from *Collected Poems*
The Estate of Siegfried Sassoon for 'At the Grave of
    Henry Vaughan' by Siegfried Sassoon
David Higham Associates Ltd for 'Still Falls the Rain' by
    Edith Sitwell, from *Collected Poems*
Michael and Anne Yeats and Macmillan London Ltd for
    'In Memory of Eva Gore-Booth and Con Markiewicz'
    by W. B. Yeats, from *Collected Poems*

Contents

Preface

'I know what I like,' said Zuleika Dobson. For this book I have chosen some of the poems which I like, though not all, for these would fill a very large volume. There are some poems here which are perhaps lesser-known, but also a few familiar favourites. I have also added notes of explanation where I thought they might be necessary. This is not a comprehensive anthology, and the poems are not all of equal merit, but I like them and, dear reader, I hope that you too will like them.

ANONYMOUS

c. 1500

Western Wind

Western wind, when will thou blow,
  The small rain down can rain?
Christ, if my love were in my arms
  And I in my bed again!

ANONYMOUS

c. 1500

Fair Helen

I wish I were where Helen lies;
Night and day on me she cries;
O that I were where Helen lies
    On fair Kirconnell lea!

Curst be the heart that thought the thought,
And curst the hand that fired the shot,
When in my arms burd Helen dropt,
    And died to succour me!

O think na but my heart was sair
When my Love dropt down and spak nae mair!
I laid her down wi' meikle care
    On fair Kirconnell lea.

As I went down the water-side,
None but my foe to be my guide,
None but my foe to be my guide,
    On fair Kirconnell lea;

I lighted down my sword to draw,
I hackèd him in pieces sma',
I hackèd him in pieces sma',
    For her sake that died for me.

O Helen fair, beyond compare!
I'll make a garland of thy hair
Shall bind my heart for evermair
    Until the day I die.

O that I were where Helen lies!
Night and day on me she cries;
Out of my bed she bids me rise,
    Says, 'Haste and come to me!'

O Helen fair! O Helen chaste!
If I were with thee, I were blest,
Where thou lies low and takes thy rest
    On fair Kirconnell lea.

I wish my grave were growing green,
A winding-sheet drawn ower my een,
And I in Helen's arms lying,
    On fair Kirconnell lea.

I wish I were where Helen lies;
Night and day on me she cries;
And I am weary of the skies,
    Since my Love died for me.

KINGSLEY AMIS
born 1922

A Bookshop Idyll

Between the GARDENING and the COOKERY
    Comes the brief POETRY shelf;
By the Nonesuch Donne, a thin anthology
    Offers itself.

Critical, and with nothing else to do,
    I scan the Contents page,
Relieved to find the names are mostly new;
    No one my age.

Like all strangers, they divide by sex:
    Landscape near Parma
Interests a man, so does *The Double Vortex*,
    So does *Rilke and Buddha*.

'I travel, you see', 'I think' and 'I can read'
    These titles seem to say;
But *I Remember You*, *Love is my Creed*,
    Poem for J.,

The ladies' choice, discountenance my patter
    For several seconds;
From somewhere in this (as in any) matter
    A moral beckons.

Should poets bicycle-pump the human heart
    Or squash it flat?
Man's love is of man's life a thing apart;
    Girls aren't like that.

We men have got love well weighed up; our stuff
    Can get by without it.
Women don't seem to think that's good enough;
    They write about it,

And the awful way their poems lay them open
    Just doesn't strike them.
Women are really much nicer than men;
    No wonder we like them.

Deciding this, we can forget those times
    We sat up half the night
Chockfull of love, crammed with bright thoughts,
        names, rhymes,
    And couldn't write.

TONY ARMSTRONG
born 1931

The Lancashire-born, Scillonian poet wrote this poem for
his little daughter.

For Bryher

We turned the green stones in search of crabs,
Your dimpled hand played the pool's serenity
And the tide came in dribs and drabs
To amuse your absolute honesty.

I found a transparent white one,
Let it crawl in your tiny palm,
Your brilliant smile in that salty sun,
Sent it scuttling up your arm.

Now you were frightened of the crab,
Tiny terror in the salty sun,
Still the tide came drib and drab
As you and the crab in fright were one.

MATTHEW ARNOLD
1822–88

The Forsaken Merman

Come, dear children, let us away;
    Down and away below.
    Now my brothers call from the bay;
Now the great winds shorewards blow;
Now the salt tides seawards flow;
Now the wild white horses play,
Champ and chafe and toss in the spray.
    Children dear, let us away!
      This way, this way!

Call her once before you go.
    Call once yet.
In a voice that she will know:
    'Margaret! Margaret!'
Children's voices should be dear
(Call once more) to a mother's ear:
Children's voices, wild with pain.
    Surely she will come again.
Call her once, and come away.
    This way, this way.
'Mother dear, we cannot stay.'
The wild white horses foam and fret.
    Margaret! Margaret!

Come, dear children, come away down.
    Call no more.
One last look at the white-walled town,
And the little grey church on the windy shore.
    Then come down.
She will not come though you call all day.
    Come away, come away!

Children dear, was it yesterday
We heard the sweet bells over the bay?
In the caverns where we lay,
Through the surf and through the swell.
The far-off sound of a silver bell?
Sand-strewn caverns, cool and deep,
Where the winds are all asleep;
Where the spent lights quiver and gleam;
Where the salt weed sways in the stream;
Where the sea-beasts, ranged all round,
Feed in the ooze of their pasture-ground;
Where the sea-snakes coil and twine,
Dry their mail and bask in the brine;
Where great whales come sailing by,
Sail and sail, with unshut eye,
Round the world for ever and aye?
When did music come this way?
Children dear, was it yesterday?

Children dear, was it yesterday
(Call yet once) that she went away?
Once she sate with you and me,
On a red gold throne in the heart of the sea,
And the youngest sate on her knee.
She combed its bright hair, and she tended it well,
When down swung the sound of the far-off bell.
She sighed, she looked up through the clear green sea.
She said: 'I must go, for my kinsfolk pray
In the little grey church on the shore to-day.
'Twill be Easter-time in the world – ah me!
And I lose my poor soul, Merman, here with thee.'
I said: 'Go up, dear heart, through the waves;
Say thy prayer, and come back to the kind sea-caves!'
She smiled, she went up through the surf in the bay.
Children dear, was it yesterday?

Children dear, were we long alone?
'The sea grows stormy, the little ones moan;
Long prayers,' I said, 'in the world they say.
Come,' I said, and we rose through the surf in the bay.

We went up the beach, by the sandy down
Where the sea-stocks bloom, to the white-walled town.
Through the narrow paved streets, where all was still,
To the little grey church on the windy hill.
From the church came a murmur of folk at their prayers,
But we stood without in the cold blowing airs.
We climbed on the graves, on the stones, worn with rains,
And we gazed up the aisle through the small leaded panes.
    She sate by the pillar; we saw her clear:
    'Margaret, hist! come quick, we are here!
    Dear heart,' I said, 'we are long alone.
    The sea grows stormy, the little ones moan.'
But, ah, she gave me never a look,
For her eyes were sealed to the holy book.
    Loud prays the priest; shut stands the door.
Come away, children, call no more!
Come away, come down, call no more!

    Down, down, down.
    Down to the depths of the sea.
She sits at her wheel in the humming town,
    Singing most joyfully.
Hark what she sings: 'O joy, O joy,
For the humming street, and the child with its toy.
For the priest, and the bell, and the holy well.
    For the wheel where I spun,
    And the blessed light of the sun!'
    And so she sings her fill,
    Singing most joyfully,
    Till the shuttle drops from her hand,
    And the whizzing wheel stands still.
She steals to the window, and looks at the sand;
    And over the sand at the sea;
    And her eyes are set in a stare;
    And anon there breaks a sigh,
    And anon there drops a tear
    From a sorrow-clouded eye,
    And a heart sorrow-laden,
    A long, long sigh

For the cold strange eyes of a little Mermaiden
    And the gleam of her golden hair.

Come away, away, children.
Come, children, come down.
The hoarse wind blows colder;
Lights shine in the town.
She will start from her slumber
When gusts shake the door;
She will hear the winds howling,
Will hear the waves roar.
We shall see, while above us
The waves roar and whirl,
A ceiling of amber,
A pavement of pearl.
Singing: 'Here came a mortal.
But faithless was she.
And alone dwell for ever
The kings of the sea.'
But, children, at midnight,
When soft the winds blow,
When clear falls the moonlight;
When spring-tides are low:
When sweet airs come seaward
From heaths starred with broom;
And high rocks throw mildly
On the blanched sands a gloom:
Up the still, glistening beeches,
Up the creeks we will hie;
Over banks of bright seaweed
The ebb-tide leaves dry.
We will gaze, from the sand-hills,
At the white, sleeping town;

At the church on the hill-side —
    And then come back down,
Singing: 'There dwells a loved one,
But cruel is she.
She left lonely for ever
The kings of the sea.'

W. H. AUDEN
1907–73

O what is that sound?

O what is that sound which so thrills the ear
   Down in the valley drumming, drumming?
Only the scarlet soldiers, dear,
         The soldiers coming.

O what is that light I see flashing so clear
   Over the distance brightly, brightly?
Only the sun on their weapons, dear,
         As they step lightly.

O what are they doing with all that gear;
   What are they doing this morning, this morning?
Only the usual manoeuvres, dear,
         Or perhaps a warning.

O why have they left the road down there;
   Why are they suddenly wheeling, wheeling?
Perhaps a change in the orders, dear;
         Why are you kneeling?

O haven't they stopped for the doctor's care;
   Haven't they reined their horses, their horses?
Why, they are none of them wounded, dear,
         None of these forces.

O is it the parson they want with white hair;
   Is it the parson, is it, is it?
No, they are passing his gateway, dear,
         Without a visit.

O it must be the farmer who lives so near;
   It must be the farmer so cunning, so cunning?
They have passed the farm already, dear,
         And now they are running.

O where are you going? stay with me here!
   Were the vows you swore me deceiving, deceiving?
No, I promised to love you, dear,
        But I must be leaving.

O it's broken the lock and splintered the door,
   O it's the gate where they're turning, turning;
Their feet are heavy on the floor
        And their eyes are burning.

JOHN BETJEMAN
born 1906

Station Syren

She sat with a Warwick Deeping,
   Her legs curl'd round in a ring,
Like a beautiful panther sleeping,
   Yet always ready to spring.

Tweed on her well-knit torso,
   Silk on each big strong leg,
An officer's lady – and more so
   Than those who buy off the peg.

More cash than she knew of for spending
   As a Southgate girl at home,
For there's crooning and clinging unending
   For the queen of the girls at the drome.

Beautiful brown eyes burning
   Deep on the Deeping page,
Beautiful dark hair learning
   Coiffuring tricks of the age.

JOHN BETJEMAN
born 1906

Sunday Morning, King's Cambridge

File into yellow candle light, fair choristers of King's
    Lost in the shadowy silence of canopied Renaissance
        stalls
In blazing glass above the dark glow skies and thrones
        and wings
    Blue, ruby, gold and green between the whiteness of
        the walls
And with what rich precision the stonework soars
        and springs
    To fountain out a spreading vault – a shower that
        never falls.

The white of windy Cambridge courts, the cobbles brown
        and dry,
    The gold of plaster Gothic with ivy overgrown,
The apple-red, the silver fronts, the wide green flats
        and high,
    The yellowing elm-trees circled out on islands of
        their own –
Oh, here behold all colours change that catch the flying sky
    To waves of pearly light that heave along the
        shafted stone.

In far East Anglian churches, the clasped hands lying long
    Recumbent on sepulchral slabs of effigied in brass
Buttress with prayer this vaulted roof so white and light
        and strong
    And countless congregations as the generations pass
Join choir and great crowned organ case, in centuries of song
    To praise Eternity contained in Time and coloured glass.

THE BIBLE

From *The Song of Solomon*

This is one of the most beautiful love poems I know. I should like to see it sung or read on the stage, by a man and a woman and a chorus, because that is how it was written.

Open to me, my sister, my love, my dove, my undefiled; for my head is filled with dew, and my locks with the drops of the night.
I rose up to my beloved; and my hands dropped with myrrh, and my fingers with sweet-smelling myrrh, upon the handles of the lock.

I don't really believe, as some Bibles suggest, that this song should be interpreted as a description of the mutual love of Christ and his church.

1

The song of songs, which *is* Solomon's.
2 Let him kiss me with the kisses of his mouth: for thy love *is* better than wine.
3 Because of the savour of thy good ointments thy name *is as* ointment poured forth, therefore do the virgins love thee.
4 Draw me, we will run after thee: the king hath brought me into his chambers: we will be glad and rejoice in thee, we will remember thy love more than wine: the upright love thee.
5 I *am* black, but comely, O ye daughters of Jerusalem, as the tents of Kedar, as the curtains of Solomon.
6 Look not upon me, because I *am* black, because the sun hath looked upon me: my mother's children were angry with me; they made me the keeper of the vineyards; *but* mine own vineyard have I not kept.
7 Tell me, O thou whom my soul loveth, where thou feedest, where thou makest *thy flock* to rest at

noon: for why should I be as one that turneth aside by the flocks of thy companions?

8 If thou know not, O thou fairest among women, go thy way forth by the footsteps of the flock, and feed thy kids beside the shepherds' tents.

9 I have compared thee, O my love, to a company of horses in Pharaoh's chariots.

10 Thy cheeks are comely with rows *of jewels*, thy neck with chains *of gold*.

11 We will make thee borders of gold with studs of silver.

12 While the king *sitteth* at this table, my spikenard sendeth forth the smell thereof.

13 A bundle of myrrh *is* my wellbeloved unto me; he shall lie all night betwixt my breasts.

14 My beloved *is* unto me *as* a cluster of camphire in the vineyards of Engedi.

15 Behold, thou *art* fair, my love; behold, thou *art* fair; thou *hast* doves' eyes.

16 Behold, thou *art* fair, my beloved, yea, pleasant: also our bed *is* green.

17 The beams of our house *are* cedar, *and* our rafters of fir.

6

10 Who *is* she *that* looketh forth as the morning, fair as the moon, clear as the sun, *and* terrible as *an army* with banners?

11 I went down into the garden of nuts to see the fruits of the valley, *and* to see whether the vine flourished, *and* the pomegranates budded.

12 Or ever I was aware, my soul made me *like* the chariots of Amminadib.

13 Return, return, O Shulamite; return, return, that we may look upon thee. What will ye see in the Shulamite? As it were the company of two armies.

7

How beautiful are thy feet with shoes, O prince's daughter! the joints of thy thighs *are* like jewels, the work of the hands of a cunning workman.

2 Thy navel *is like* a round goblet, *which* wanteth not liquor: thy belly *is like* an heap of wheat set about with lilies.

3 Thy two breasts *are* like two young roes *that are* twins.

4 Thy neck *is* as a tower of ivory; thine eyes *like* the fishpools in Heshbon, by the gate of Bath-rabbim: thy nose *is* as the tower of Lebanon which looketh toward Damascus.

5 Thine head upon thee *is* like Carmel, and the hair of thine head like purple; the king *is* held in the galleries.

6 How fair and how pleasant art thou, O love, for delights!

7 This thy stature is like to a palm tree, and thy breasts to clusters *of grapes*.

8 I said, I will go up to the palm tree, I will take hold of the boughs thereof: now also thy breasts shall be as clusters of the vine, and the smell of thy nose like apples;

9 And the roof of thy mouth like the best wine for my beloved, that goeth *down* sweetly, causing the lips of those that are asleep to speak.

10 I *am* my beloved's, and his desire *is* toward me.

11 Come, my beloved, let us go forth into the field; let us lodge in the villages.

12 Let us get up early to the vineyards; let us see if the vine flourish, *whether* the tender grapes appear, *and* the pomegranates bud forth: there will I give thee my loves.

13 The mandrakes give a smell, and at our gates *are* all manner of pleasant *fruits*, new and old, *which* I have laid up for thee. O my beloved.

8

O that thou *wert* as my brother, that sucked the breasts of my mother! *when* I should find thee

without, I would kiss thee; yea, I should not be
despised.

2 I would lead thee, *and* bring thee into my
mother's house, *who* would instruct me: I would
cause thee to drink of spiced wine of the juice
of my pomegranate.

3 His left hand *should be* under my head, and his
right hand should embrace me.

4 I charge you, O daughters of Jerusalem, that
ye stir not up, nor awake *my* love, until he
please.

5 Who *is* this that cometh up from the wilderness,
leaning upon her beloved? I raised thee up under
the apple tree: there thy mother brought thee forth:
there she brought thee forth *that* bare
thee.

6 Set me as a seal upon thine heart, as a seal upon
thine arm: for love *is* strong as death; jealousy *is*
cruel as the grave: the coals thereof *are* coals of fire,
which hath a most vehement flame.

7 Many waters cannot quench love, neither can the
floods drown it: if a man would give all the
substance of his house for love, it would utterly be
contemned.

8 We have a little sister, and she hath no breasts:
what shall we do for our sister in the day when she
shall be spoken for?

9 If she *be* a wall, we will build upon her a palace of
silver: and if she *be* a door, we will inclose her with
boards of cedar.

10 I *am* a wall, and my breasts like towers: then was I
in his eyes as one that found favour.

11 Solomon had a vineyard at Baalhamon; he let
out the vineyard unto keepers; every one for the
fruit thereof was to bring a thousand *pieces* of
silver.

12 My vineyard, which *is* mine, *is* before me: thou,
O Solomon, *must have* a thousand, and those that
keep the fruit thereof two hundred.

13 Thou that dwellest in the gardens, the companions hearken to thy voice: cause me to hear *it*.

14 Make haste, my beloved, and be thou like to a roe or to a young hart upon the mountains of spices.

WILLIAM BLAKE
1757–1827

Nurse's Song

When the voices of children are heard on the green
And laughing is heard on the hill,
My heart is at rest within my breast
And everything else is still

Then come home my children, the sun is gone down
And the dews of night arise
Come come leave off play, and let us away
Till the morning appears in the skies

No no let us play, for it is yet day
And we cannot go to sleep
Besides in the sky, the little birds fly
And the hills are all covered with sheep

Well well go & play till the light fades away
And then go home to bed
The little ones leaped & shouted & laugh'd
And all the hills echoed

GORDON BOTTOMLEY
1874–1948

To Iron-Founders and Others

When you destroy a blade of grass
You poison England at her roots:
Remember no man's foot can pass
Where evermore no green life shoots.

You force the birds to wing too high
Where your unnatural vapours creep:
Surely the living rocks shall die
When birds no rightful distance keep.

You have brought down the firmament
And yet no heaven is more near;
You shape huge deeds without event,
And half-made men believe and fear.

Your worship is your furnaces,
Which, like old idols, lost obscenes,
Have molten bowels; your vision is
Machines for making more machines.

O, you are busied in the night,
Preparing destinies of rust;
Iron misused must turn to blight
And dwindle to a tetter'd crust.

ROBERT BRIDGES
1844–1930

I will not let thee go

I will not let thee go.
Ends all our month-long love in this?
Can it be summed up so,
Quit in a single kiss?
I will not let thee go.

I will not let thee go.
If thy words' breath could scare thy deeds,
As the soft south can blow
And toss the feathered seeds,
Then might I let thee go.

I will not let thee go.
Had not the great sun seen, I might;
Or were he reckoned slow
To bring the false to light,
Then might I let thee go.

I will not let thee go.
The stars that crowd the summer skies
Have watched us so below
With all their million eyes,
I dare not let thee go.

I will not let thee go.
Have we not chid the changeful moon,
Now rising late, and now
Because she set too soon,
And shall I let thee go?

I will not let thee go.
Have not the young flowers been content,
　　Plucked ere their buds could blow,
　　To seal our sacrament?
　　I cannot let thee go.

　　I will not let thee go.
I hold thee by too many bands:
　　Thou sayest farewell, and lo!
　　I have thee by the hands,
　　And will not let thee go.

EMILY BRONTË
1818–48

Last Lines

No coward soul is mine,
No trembler in the world's storm troubled sphere:
    I see Heaven's glories shine,
And faith shines equal, arming me from fear.

O God within my breast,
Almighty, ever-present Deity!
    Life – that in me has rest,
As I – undying Life – have power in Thee!

Vain are the thousand creeds
That move men's hearts: unutterably vain;
    Worthless as withered weeds,
Or idlest froth amid the boundless main,

To waken doubt in one
Holding so fast by Thine infinity;
    So surely anchored on
The steadfast rock of immortality.

With wide-embracing love
Thy Spirit animates eternal years,
    Pervades and broods above,
Changes, sustains, dissolves, creates, and rears.

Though earth and man were gone,
And suns and universes ceased to be,
    And Thou were left alone,
Every existence would exist in Thee.

There is not room for Death,
Nor atom that his might could render void:
    Thou – THOU art Being and Breath,
And what THOU art may never be destroyed.

EMILY BRONTË
1818–48

Remembrance

Cold in the earth – and the deep snow piled above thee,
Far, far, removed, cold in the dreary grave!
Have I forgot, my only Love, to love thee,
Severed at last by Time's all-severing wave?

Now, when alone, do my thoughts no longer hover
Over the mountains, on that northern shore,
Resting their wings where heath and fern-leaves cover
Thy noble heart for ever, ever more?

Cold in the earth – and fifteen wild Decembers,
From those brown hills, have melted into spring:
Faithful, indeed, is the spirit that remembers
After such years of change and suffering!

Sweet Love of youth, forgive, if I forget thee,
While the world's tide is bearing me along;
Other desires and other hopes beset me,
Hopes which obscure, but cannot do thee wrong!

No later light has lightened up my heaven,
No second morn has ever shone for me;
All my life's bliss from thy dear life was given,
All my life's bliss is in the grave with thee.

But, when the days of golden dreams had perished,
And even Despair was powerless to destroy;
Then did I learn how existence could be cherished,
Strengthened and fed without the aid of joy.

Then did I check the tears of useless passion –
Weaned my young soul from yearning after thine;
Sternly denied its burning wish to hasten
Down to that tomb already more than mine.

And, even yet, I dare not let it languish,
Dare not indulge in memory's rapturous pain;
Once drinking deep of that divinest anguish,
How could I seek the empty world again?

EMILY BRONTË
1818–48

The Prisoner

Still let my tyrants know, I am not doomed to wear
Year after year in gloom, and desolate despair;
A messenger of Hope comes every night to me,
And offers for short life, eternal liberty.

He comes with western winds, with evening's wandering airs,
With that clear dusk of heaven that brings the thickest stars,
Winds take a pensive tone, and stars a tender fire,
And visions rise, and change, that kill me with desire.

Desire for nothing known in my maturer years,
When Joy grew mad with awe, at counting future tears.
When, if my spirit's sky was full of flashes warm,
I knew not whence they came, from sun or thunder-storm.

But, first, a hush of peace – a soundless calm descends;
The struggle of distress, and fierce impatience ends;
Mute music soothes my breast – unuttered harmony,
That I could never dream, till Earth was lost to me.

Then dawns the Invisible; the Unseen its truth reveals;
My outward sense is gone, my inward essence feels:
Its wings are almost free – its home, its harbour found,
Measuring the gulf, it stoops and dares the final bound.

O! dreadful is the check – intense the agony –
When the ear begins to hear, and the eye begins to see;
When the pulse begins to throb, the brain to think again;
The soul to feel the flesh, and the flesh to feel the chain.

Yet I would lose no sting, would wish no torture less;
The more that anguish racks, the earlier it will bless;
And robed in fires of hell, or bright with heavenly shine,
If it but herald death, the vision is divine!

ELIZABETH BARRETT BROWNING
1806–61

A Musical Instrument

What was he doing, the great god Pan,
  Down in the reeds by the river?
Spreading ruin and scattering ban,
Splashing and paddling with hoofs of a goat,
And breaking the golden lilies afloat
  With the dragon-fly on the river.

He tore out a reed, the great god Pan,
  From the deep cool bed of the river:
The limpid water turbidly ran,
And the broken lilies a-dying lay,
And the dragon-fly had fled away,
  Ere he brought it out of the river.

High on the shore sate the great god Pan,
  While turbidly flowed the river;
And hacked and hewed as a great god can,
With his hard bleak steel at the patient reed,
Till there was not a sign of a leaf indeed
  To prove it fresh from the river.

He cut it short, did the great god Pan
  (How tall it stood in the river!),
Then drew the pith, like the heart of a man,
Steadily from the outside ring,
And notched the poor dry empty thing
  In holes, as he sate by the river.

'This is the way,' laughed the great god Pan
  (Laughed while he sate by the river),
'The only way, since gods began
To make sweet music, they could succeed.'
Then, dropping his mouth to a hole in the reed,
  He blew in power by the river.

Sweet, sweet, sweet, O Pan!
  Piercing sweet by the river!
Blinding sweet, O great god Pan!
The sun on the hill forgot to die,
And the lilies revived, and the dragon-fly
  Came back to dream on the river.

Yet half a beast is the great god Pan,
  To laugh as he sits by the river,
Making a poet out of a man:
The true gods sigh for the cost and pain –
For the reed which grows nevermore again
  As a reed with the reeds in the river.

ROBERT BROWNING

1812–90

Porphyria's Lover

The rain set early in to-night,
   The sullen wind was soon awake,
It tore the elm-tops down for spite,
   And did its worst to vex the lake:
   I listened with heart fit to break.
When glided in Porphyria; straight
   She shut the cold out and the storm,
And kneeled and made the cheerless grate
   Blaze up, and all the cottage warm;
   Which done, she rose, and from her form
Withdrew the dripping cloak and shawl,
   And laid her soiled gloves by, untied
Her hat and let the damp hair fall,
   And, last, she sat down by my side
   And called me. When no voice replied,
She put my arm about her waist,
   And made her smooth white shoulder bare,
And all her yellow hair displaced,
   And stooping, made my cheek lie there,
   And spread, o'er all, her yellow hair,
Murmuring how she loved me – she
   Too weak, for all her heart's endeavour,
To set its struggling passion free
   From pride, and vainer ties dissever,
   And give herself to me for ever.
But passion sometimes would prevail,
   Nor could to-night's gay feast restrain
A sudden thought of one so pale
   For love of her, and all in vain:
   So, she was come through wind and rain,
Be sure I looked up at her eyes

Happy and proud; at last I knew
Porphyria worshipped me; surprise
    Made my heart swell, and still it grew
    While I debated what to do.

That moment she was mine, mine, fair,
    Perfectly pure and good: I found
A thing to do, and all her hair
    In one long yellow string I wound
    Three times her little throat around,
And strangled her. No pain felt she;
    I am quite sure she felt no pain.
As a shut bud that holds the bee,
    I warily oped her lids: again
    Laughed the blue eyes without a stain.
And I untightened next the tress
    About her neck; her cheek once more
Blushed bright beneath my burning kiss
    I propped her head up as before,
    Only, this time my shoulder bore
Her head, which droops upon it still:
    The smiling rosy little head,
So glad it has its utmost will,
    That all it scorned at once is fled,
    And I, its love, am gained instead!
Porphyria's love: she guessed not how
    Her darling one wish would be heard.
And thus we sit together now,
    And all night long we have not stirred,
    And yet God has not said a word!

ROBERT BURNS
1759–96

Song: *My luve is like a red, red rose*

This is one of the best-known poems in the language; I
find it striking because it contains only seven words of
more than one syllable – it is beautifully simple.

My luve is like a red, red rose
   That's newly sprung in June:
My luve is like the melodie
   That's sweetly played in tune.

As fair thou art, my bonnie lass,
   So deep in luve am I:
And I will luve thee still, my dear,
   Till a' the seas gang dry.

Till a' the seas gang dry, my dear,
   And the rocks melt wi' the sun:
I will luve thee still, my dear,
   While the sands o' life shall run.

And fare thee weel, my only luve!
   And fare thee weel awhile!
And I will come again, my luve,
   Tho' it were ten thousand mile.

LORD BYRON

1798–1824

There be none of Beauty's daughters

There be none of Beauty's daughters
　　With a magic like Thee;
And like music on the waters
　　Is thy sweet voice to me:
When, as if its sound were causing
The charmed ocean's pausing,
The waves lie still and gleaming,
And the lull'd winds seem dreaming:

And the midnight moon is weaving
　　Her bright chain o'er the deep,
Whose breast is gently heaving
　　As an infant's asleep:
So the spirit bows before thee
To listen and adore thee;
With a full but soft emotion,
Like the swell of Summer's ocean.

THOMAS CAMPBELL

1777–1844

Lord Ullin's Daughter

This very well-known and tragic poem interests me and,
I'm afraid, amuses me, because I like the characters: the
yielding un-named daughter, the terrified suitor, the
stern and soft-hearted father. I think I like the boatman
best – a brave man with an eye for a pretty girl.

A Chieftain to the Highlands bound
Cries 'Boatman, do not tarry!
And I'll give thee a silver pound
To row us o'er the ferry!'

'Now who be ye, would cross Lochgyle,
This dark and stormy water?'
'O I'm the chief of Ulva's isle,
And this, Lord Ullin's daughter.

'And fast before her father's men
Three days we've fled together,
For should he find us in the glen,
My blood would stain the heather.

'His horsemen hard behind us ride –
Should they our steps discover,
Then who will cheer my bonny bride,
When they have slain her lover?'

Out spoke the hardy Highland wight,
'I'll go, my chief, I'm ready:
It is not for your silver bright,
But for your winsome lady:–

'And by my word! the bonny bird
In danger shall not tarry;
So though the waves are raging white
I'll row you o'er the ferry.'

By this the storm grew loud apace,
The water-wraith was shrieking;
And in the scowl of Heaven each face
Grew dark as they were speaking.

But still as wilder blew the wind,
And as the night grew drearer,
Adown the glen rode armèd men,
Their trampling sounded nearer.

'O haste thee, haste!' the lady cries,
'Though tempests round us gather;
I'll meet the raging of the skies,
But not an angry father.'

The boat has left a stormy land,
A stormy sea before her, –
When, oh! too strong for human hand
The tempest gather'd o'er her.

And still they row'd amidst the roar
Of waters fast prevailing:
Lord Ullin reach'd that fatal shore, –
His wrath was changed to wailing.

For, sore dismay'd, through storm and shade
His child he did discover:–
One lovely hand she stretch'd for aid.
And one was round her lover.

'Come back! come back!' he cried in grief,
'Across this stormy water:
And I'll forgive your Highland chief,
My daughter! – Oh, my daughter!'

'Twas vain: the loud waves lash'd the shore,
Return or aid preventing:
The waters wild went o'er his child,
And he was left lamenting.

G. K. CHESTERTON
1872–1936

The Last Hero

The wind blew out from Bergen from the dawning to the day,
There was a wreck of trees and fall of towers a score of miles
      away,
And drifted like a livid leaf I go before its tide,
Spewed out of house and stable, beggared of flag and bride.
The heavens are bowed about my head, shouting like seraph
      wars,
With rains that might put out the sun and clean the sky of
      stars,
Rains like the fall of ruined seas from secret worlds above,
The roaring of the rains of God none but the lonely love.
Feast in my hall, O foemen, and eat and drink and drain,
You never loved the sun in heaven as I have loved the rain.

The chance of battle changes – so may all battle be;
I stole my lady bride from them, they stole her back from me.
I rent her from her red-roofed hall, I rode and saw arise
More lovely than the living flowers the hatred in her eyes.
She never loved me, never bent, never was less divine;
The sunset never loved me; the wind was never mine.
Was it all nothing that she stood imperial in duresse?
Silence itself made softer with the sweeping of her dress.
O you who drain the cup of life, O you who wear the crown,
You never loved a woman's smile as I have loved her frown.

The wind blew out from Bergen from the dawning to the day,
They ride and run with fifty spears to break and bar my way,
I shall not die alone, alone, but kin to all the powers,
As merry as the ancient sun and fighting like the flowers.
How white their steel, how bright their eyes! I love each
      laughing knave,

Cry high and bid him welcome to the banquet of the brave.
Yea, I will bless them as they bend and love them where they
      lie,
When on their skulls the sword I swing falls shattering
        from the sky.
The hour when death is like a light and blood is like a rose, –
You never loved your friends, my friends, as I shall love my
      foes.

Know you what earth shall lose to-night, what rich
        uncounted loans,
What heavy gold of tales untold you bury with my bones?
My loves in deep dim meadows, my ships that rode at ease,
Ruffling the purple plumage of strange and secret seas.
To see this fair earth as it is to me alone was given,
The blow that breaks my brow to-night shall break
        the dome of heaven.
The skies I saw, the trees I saw after no eyes shall see.
To-night I die the death of God: the stars shall die with me:
One sound shall sunder all the spears and break
        the trumpet's breath:
You never laughed in all your life as I shall laugh in death.

JOHN CLARE
1793–1864

From *December*

Thou day of happy sound and mirth
That long wi childish memory stays
How blest around the cottage hearth
I met thee in my boyish days
Harping wi raptures dreaming joys
On presents that thy coming found
The welcome sight of little toys
The christmass gifts of comers round

The wooden horse wi arching head
Drawn upon wheels around the room
The gilded coach of ginger bread
And many colord sugar plumb
Gilt coverd books for pictures sought
Or storys childhood loves to tell
Wi many a urgent promise bought
To get tomorrows lesson well

And many a thing a minutes sport
Left broken on the sanded floor
When we woud leave our play and court
Our parents promises for more
Tho manhood bids such raptures dye
And throws such toys away as vain
Yet memory loves to turn her eye
And talk such pleasures oer again

Around the glowing hearth at night
The harmless laugh and winter tale
Goes round – while parting friends delight
To toast each other oer their ale
The cotter oft wi quiet zeal
Will musing oer his bible lean
While in the dark the lovers steal
To kiss and toy behind the screen

The yule cake dotted thick wi plumbs
Is on each supper table found
And cats look up for falling crumbs
Which greedy children litter round
And huswifes sage stuffd seasond chine
Long hung in chimney nook to drye
And boiling eldern berry wine
To drink the christmass eves 'good bye'

ARTHUR HUGH CLOUGH
1819–61

Say not the struggle naught availeth

This poem is so well known that I hesitated before including it; but to the generation which remembers the Second
World War it has a special meaning. Winston Churchill
quoted the last verse in a speech which he made just
before the USA's entry into the war: 'But westward, look,
the land is bright!'

> Say not the struggle naught availeth,
>   The labour and the wounds are vain,
> The enemy faints not, nor faileth,
>   And as things have been they remain.
>
> If hopes were dupes, fears may be liars;
>   It may be, in yon smoke concealed,
> Your comrades chase e'en now the fliers,
>   And, but for you, possess the field.
>
> For while the tired waves, vainly breaking,
>   Seem here no painful inch to gain,
> Far back, through creeks and inlets making,
>   Comes silent, flooding in, the main.
>
> And not by eastern windows only,
>   When daylight comes, comes in the light,
> In front, the sun climbs slow, how slowly,
>   But westward, look, the land is bright!

PADRAIC COLUM
1881–1972

She Moved through the Fair

My young love said to me, 'My brothers won't mind,
And my parents won't slight you for your lack of kind.'
Then she stepped away from me, and this she did say,
'It will not be long, love, till our wedding day.'

She stepped away from me and she moved through the fair,
And fondly I watched her go here and go there,
Then she went her way homeward with one star awake,
As the swan in the evening moves over the lake.

The people were saying no two were e'er wed
But one had a sorrow that never was said,
And I smiled as she passed with her goods and her gear,
And that was the last that I saw of my dear.

I dreamt it last night that my young love came in,
So softly she entered, her feet made no din;
She came close beside me, and this she did say,
'It will not be long, love, till our wedding day.'

WALTER DE LA MARE
1873–1956

Nod

Softly along the road of evening,
  In a twilight dim with rose,
Wrinkled with age, and drenched with dew
  Old Nod, the shepherd, goes.

His drowsy flock streams on before him,
  Their fleeces charged with gold,
To where the sun's last beam leans low
  On Nod the shepherd's fold.

The hedge is quick and green with briar,
  From their sand the conies creep;
And all the birds that fly in heaven
  Flock singing home to sleep.

His lambs outnumber a noon's roses,
  Yet, when night's shadows fall,
His blind old sheep-dog, Slumber-soon,
  Misses not one of all.

His are the quiet steeps of dreamland,
  The waters of no-more-pain,
His ram's bell rings 'neath an arch of stars,
  'Rest, rest, and rest again.'

WALTER DE LA MARE
1873–1956

Fare Well

When I lie where shades of darkness
Shall no more assail mine eyes,
Nor the rain make lamentation
    When the wind sighs;
How will fare the world whose wonder
Was the very proof of me?
Memory fades, must the remember'd
    Perishing be?

Oh, when this my dust surrenders
Hand, foot, lip, to dust again,
May these loved and loving faces
    Please other men!
May the rusting harvest hedgerow
Still the Traveller's Joy entwine,
And as happy children gather
    Posies once mine.

Look thy last on all things lovely,
Every hour. Let no night
Seal thy sense in deathly slumber
    Till to delight
Thou have paid thy utmost blessing,
Since that all things thou wouldst praise
Beauty took from those who loved them
    In other days.

DIGBY MACKWORTH DOLBEN
1848–67

This poet died by drowning at a tragically early age. There
is a portrait on the cover of his *Uncollected Poems* – he had
one of the most beautiful faces I have ever seen.

Oh Love, first Love

Oh Love, first love, comes gently through the wood,
Gently crushing the snowdrops as he goes;
Relics of winter fade from out his path,
And all around with crocus radiance glows.
  The wintry winds have blown themselves away,
  Clear are the skies, and fragrant is the air,
  The purest beams a rising sun can give
  Play in the waving glory of his hair.

Ah Love, first Love, came gently through the wood,
Under a tree he found me all alone,
Gently, gently, he kissed me on the cheek,
And gently took my hand within his own.
  Loudly, loudly the birds above us sang,
  Brightly, brightly the sun above us shone,
  Hand in hand we wandered through the flowers,
  And so the spring to midsummer passed on.

The golden radiance is faded from our path,
And that sweet wood we can enter nevermore;
No flowery carpet lies beneath our feet,
But a waste of thicket and of dreary moor.
  But still his hand is clasped within my own,
  So, whether we wander through desert or through brake,
  The sharpest briars and the roughest stones
  Are ever dear to me for his dear sake.

JOHN DONNE
1573–1631

Elegy XIX

To his Mistress going to Bed

Come, Madam, come, all rest my powers defy,
Until I labour, I in labour lie.
The foe oft-times having the foe in sight,
Is tired with standing though he never fight.
Off with that girdle, like heaven's Zone glistering,
But a far fairer world encompassing.
Unpin that spangled breastplate which you wear.
That th' eyes of busy fools may be stopt there.
Unlace yourself, for that harmonious chime
Tells me from you, that now it is bed time.
Off with that happy busk, which I envy,
That still can be, and still can stand so nigh.
Your gown going off, such beauteous state reveals,
As when from flowry meads th' hill's shadow steals.
Off with that wiry Coronet and show
The hairy Diadem which on you doth grow:
Now off with those shoes, and then safely tread
In this love's hallow'd temple, this soft bed.
In such white robes, heaven's Angels used to be
Receiv'd by men; thou Angel bring'st with thee
A heaven like Mahomet's Paradise; and though
Ill spirits walk in white, we easily know,
By this these Angels from an evil sprite,
Those set our hairs, but these our flesh upright.
  Licence my roving hands, and let them go,
Before, behind, between, above, below.
O my America! my new-found-land,
My kingdom, safeliest when with one man mann'd,
My Mine of precious stones, My Empery,
How blest am I in this discovering thee!
To enter in these bonds, is to be free;
Then where my hand is set, my seal shall be.

Full nakedness! All joys are due to thee,
As souls unbodied, bodies uncloth'd must be,
To taste whole joys. Gems which you women use
Are like Atlanta's balls, cast in men's views,
That when a fool's eye lighteth on a Gem,
His earthly soul may covet theirs, not them.
Like pictures, or like books' gay coverings made
For lay-men, are all women thus array'd;
Themselves are mystic books, which only we
(Whom their imputed grace will dignify)
Must see reveal'd. Then since that I may know,
As liberally, as to a Midwife, show
Thyself: cast all, yea, this white linen hence,
There is no penance due to innocence.
    To teach thee, I am naked first; why then
What needst thou have more covering than a man.

LORD ALFRED DOUGLAS
1870–1945

The Dead Poet

I dreamed of him last night, I saw his face
All radiant and unshadowed of distress,
And as of old, in music measureless,
I heard his golden voice and marked him trace
Under the common thing the hidden grace,
And conjure wonder out of emptiness,
Till mean things put on beauty like a dress
And all the world was an enchanted place.

And then methought outside a fast locked gate
I mourned the loss of unrecorded words,
Forgotten tales and mysteries half said,
Wonders that might have been articulate,
And voiceless thoughts like murdered singing birds.
And so I woke and knew that he was dead.

JOHN DRINKWATER
1882–1937

In Lady Street

All day long the traffic goes
In Lady Street by dingy rows
Of sloven houses, tattered shops –
Fried fish, old clothes and fortune-tellers –
Tall trams on silver-shining rails,
With grinding wheels and swaying tops,
And lorries with their corded bales,
And screeching cars. 'Buy, buy!' the sellers
Of rags and bones and sickening meat
Cry all day long in Lady Street.

And when the sunshine has its way
In Lady Street, then all the grey
Dull desolation grows in state
More dull and grey and desolate,
And the sun is a shamefast thing,
A lord not comely-housed, a god
Seeing what gods must blush to see,
A song where it is ill to sing,
And each gold ray despiteously
Lies like a gold ironic rod.

Yet one grey man in Lady Street
Looks for the sun. He never bent
Life to his will, his travelling feet
Have scaled no cloudy continent,
Nor has the sickle-hand been strong.
He lives in Lady Street; a bed,
Four cobwebbed walls.

                    But all day long
A time is singing in his head
Of youth in Gloucester lanes. He hears
The wind among the barley-blades,
The tapping of the woodpeckers
On the smooth beeches, thistle-spades
Slicing the sinewy roots; he sees
The hooded filberts in the copse
Beyond the loaded orchard trees,
The netted avenues of hops;
He smells the honeysuckle thrown
Along the hedge. He lives alone,
Alone – yet not alone, for sweet
Are Gloucester lanes in Lady Street.

Aye, Gloucester lanes. For down below
The cobwebbed room this grey man plies
A trade, a coloured trade. A show
Of many-coloured merchandise
Is in his shop. Brown filberts there,
And apples red with Gloucester air,
And cauliflowers he keeps, and round
Smooth marrows grown on Gloucester ground,
Fat cabbages and yellow plums,
And gaudy brave chrysanthemums.
And times a glossy pheasant lies
Among his store, not Tyrian dyes
More rich than are the neck-feathers;
And times a prize of violets,
Or dewy mushrooms satin-skinned
And times an unfamiliar wind
Robbed of its woodland favour stirs
Gay daffodils this grey man sets
Among his treasure.

                    All day long
In Lady Street the traffic goes
By dingy houses, desolate rows
Of shops that stare like hopeless eyes.
Day long the sellers cry their cries,
The fortune-tellers tell no wrong.

Of lives that know not any right,
And drift, that has not even the will
To drift, toils through the day until
The wage of sleep is won at night.
But this grey man heeds not at all
The hell of Lady Street. His stall
Of many-coloured merchandise
He makes a shining paradise,
As all day long chrysanthemums
He sells, and red and yellow plums
And cauliflowers. In that one spot
Of Lady Street the sun is not
Ashamed to shine and send a rare
Shower of colour through the air;
The grey man says the sun is sweet
On Gloucester lanes in Lady Street.

WILLIAM DUNBAR
?1460–1520

Timor Mortis Conturbat Me

I that in heill wes and gladnes
Am trublit now with gret seiknes
And feblit with infirmite:
    Timor mortis conturbat me.

Our plesance here is all vane glory,
This fals warld is bot transitory,
The flesche is brukle, the Fend is sle:
    Timor mortis conturbat me.

The stait of man dois change and vary,
Now sound, now seik, now blith, now sary,
Now dansand mery, now like to dee:
    Timor mortis conturbat me.

No stait in erd heir standis sickir;
As with the wynd wavis the wickir
Wavis this warldis vanite:
    Timor mortis conturbat me.

On to the ded gois all estatis,
Princis, prelotis, and potestatis,
Baith riche and pur of all degre:
    Timor mortis conturbat me.

He takis the knychtis in to feild,
Anarmit under helme and scheild;
Victour he is at all mellie:
    Timor mortis conturbat me.

Timor mortis conturbat me: The fear of Death troubles me (Office of the Dead);
brukle: feeble; sle: cunning; sickir: sure; wickir: willow.

T. S. ELIOT

1888–1965

Journey of the Magi

'A cold coming we had of it,
Just the worst time of the year
For a journey, and such a long journey:
The ways deep and the weather sharp,
The very dead of winter.'
And the camels galled, sore-footed, refractory,
Lying down in the melting snow.
There were times we regretted
The summer palaces on slopes, the terraces,
And the silken girls bringing sherbet.
Then the camel men cursing and grumbling
And running away, and wanting their liquor and women,
And the night-fires going out, and the lack of shelters,
And the cities hostile and the towns unfriendly
And the villages dirty and charging high prices:
A hard time we had of it.
At the end we preferred to travel all night,
Sleeping in snatches,
With the voices singing in our ears, saying
That this was all folly.

Then at dawn we came down to a temperate valley,
Wet, below the snow line, smelling of vegetation;
With a running stream and a water-mill beating the darkness,
And three trees on the low sky,
And an old white horse galloped away in the meadow.
Then we came to a tavern with vine-leaves over the lintel,
Six hands at an open door dicing for pieces of silver,
And feet kicking the empty wine-skins.
But there was no information, and so we continued
And arrived at evening, not a moment too soon
Finding the place; it was (you may say) satisfactory.

All this was a long time ago, I remember,
And I would do it again, but set down
This set down
This: were we led all that way for
Birth or Death? There was a Birth, certainly,
We had evidence and no doubt. I had seen birth and death,
But had thought they were different; this birth was
Hard and bitter agony for us, like Death, our death.
We returned to our places, these Kingdoms,
But no longer at ease here, in the old dispensation,
With an alien people clutching their gods.
I should be glad of another death.

JAMES ELROY FLECKER
1884–1919

The Old Ships

I have seen old ships sail like swans asleep
Beyond the village which men still call Tyre,
With leaden age o'ercargoed, dipping deep
For Famagusta and the hidden sun
That rings black Cyprus with a lake of fire;
And all those ships were certainly so old
Who knows how oft with squat and noisy gun,
Questing brown slaves or Syrian oranges,
The pirate Genoese
Hell-raked them till they rolled
Blood, water, fruit and corpses up the hold.
But now through friendly seas they softly run,
Painted the mid-sea blue or shore-sea green,
Still patterned with the vine and grapes in gold.

But I have seen,
Pointing her shapely shadows from the dawn
And image tumbled on a rose-swept bay,
A drowsy ship of some yet older day;
And, wonder's breath indrawn,
Thought I – who knows – who knows – but in that same
(Fished up beyond Æœa, patched up new
– Stern painted brighter blue –)
That talkative, bald-headed seaman came
(Twelve patient comrades sweating at the oar)
From Troy's doom-crimson shore,
And with great lies about his wooden horse
Set the crew laughing, and forgot his course.

It was so old a ship – who knows, who knows?
– And yet so beautiful, I watched in vain
To see the mast burst open with a rose,
And the whole deck put on its leaves again.

H. W. GARROD
1878–1960

A 'Bump Supper'

So ends your week: six bumps in all:
　　Why, take your pleasure and be done:
Shake with your shouting every wall,
　　And stir with stamping every stone.

Those stones have stood six hundred years,
　　And looked perchance on ruder joys:
The feet of careless Cavaliers
　　Beat on them once as brave a noise.

To trumpet's blare or tramp of feet,
　　Be sure, they will not fall to-night,
Nor the weak cymbals that you beat
　　Loosen their immemorial might.

They stand forever; and their eyes
　　Through all the ages never sleep,
But ever over joy that dies
　　A vain and bitter vigil keep.

RICHARD M. GOMM
born 1953

This poet suffers from cerebral palsy, but in spite of his disabilities he went to university and is now reading for a PhD. These two poems are taken from his book *The Seasons of my Life*, published by Mitre Press.

Winter Sunset

Now as tinted clouds cross the sun –
Like so many golden-fleeced sheep
Wending their way wearily home,
midst the dying day –
My thoughts also turn homewards . . .
But, although my home is full of
bright light and blazing log-fires,
Full of Keats, McKuen, Picasso and Bach
to keep out the cold, long, lonely winter nights,
It lacks a most precious being;
a warm, a very beautiful person:
you.

RICHARD M. GOMM
born 1953

Leaf

Amongst old letters
I found a pressed
Red-oak leaf –
A hope once, but now forgotten.
Like the faded words on the paper.
Yet no memories did it evoke;
Somebody sent it
Before you came.

GERALD GOULD
1885–1936

Some readers may feel that this book is overloaded with
poems about Oxford; if so, I can only apologise and say
that, of the hundreds of poems written about that beautiful city, I have included just a few of my favourites.

Oxford

I came to Oxford in the light
   Of a spring-coloured afternoon;
Some clouds were grey and some were white,
   And all were blown to such a tune
Of quiet rapture in the sky,
I laughed to see them laughing by.

I had been dreaming in the train
   With thoughts at random from my book;
I looked, and read, and looked again,
   And suddenly to greet my look
Oxford shone up with every tower
Aspiring sweetly like a flower.

Home turn the feet of men that seek,
   And home the hearts of children turn,
And none can teach the hour to speak
   What every hour is free to learn;
And all discover, late or soon
Their golden Oxford afternoon.

H. RIDER HAGGARD
1856–1925

This poem is the tailpiece to Rider Haggard's novel, *She*.

She

To H.R.H.

Not in the waste beyond the swamps and sand,
   The fever-haunted forest and lagoon,
Mysterious Kôr thy walls forsaken stand,
   Thy lonely towers beneath the lonely moon –
   Not there doth Ayesha linger, rune by rune –
Spelling strange scriptures of a people banned.
The world is disenchanted: over soon
Shall Europe send her spies through all the land.

Nay, not in Kôr, but in whatever spot,
   In town or field, or by the insatiate sea,
Men brood on buried loves and unforgot
   Or break themselves on some Divine decree,
   Or would o'erleap the limits of their lot –
   There, in the tombs and deathless, dwelleth SHE.

THOMAS HARDY
1840–1928

The Workbox

'See, here's the workbox, little wife,
   That I made of polished oak.'
He was a joiner, of village life;
   She came of borough folk.

He holds the present up to her
   As with a smile she nears
And answers to the profferer,
   ''Twill last all my sewing years!'

'I warrant it will. And longer too.
   'Tis a scantling that I got
Off poor John Wayward's coffin, who
   Died of they knew not what.

'The shingled pattern that seems to cease
   Against your box's rim
Continues right on in the piece
   That's underground with him.

'And while I worked it made me think
   Of timber's varied doom;
One inch where people eat and drink,
   The next inch in a tomb.

'But why do you look so white, my dear,
   And turn aside your face?
You knew not that good lad, I fear,
   Though he came from your native place?'

'How could I know that good young man,
   Though he came from my native town,
When he must have left far earlier than
   I was a woman grown?'

'Ah, no. I should have understood!
    It shocked you that I gave
To you one end of a piece of wood
    Whose other is in a grave?'

'Don't, dear, despise my intellect,
    Mere accidental things
Or that sort never have effect
    On my imaginings.'

Yet still her lips were limp and wan,
    Her face still held aside,
As if she had known not only John,
    But known of what he died.

THOMAS HARDY
1840–1928

Afterwards

When the Present has latched its postern behind my
    tremulous stay,
  And the May month flaps its glad green leaves like wings,
Delicate-filmed as new-spun silk, will the neighbours say,
  'He was a man who used to notice such things'?

If it be in the dusk when, like an eyelid's soundless blink,
  The dewfall-hawk comes crossing the shades to alight
Upon the wind-warped upland thorn, a gazer may think,
  'To him this must have been a familiar sight.'

If I pass during some nocturnal blackness, mothy and warm,
  When the hedgehog travels furtively over the lawn,
One may say, 'He strove that such innocent creatures
    should come to no harm,
  But he could do little for them; and now he is gone.'

If, when hearing that I have been stilled at last, they stand at
    the door,
  Watching the full-starred heavens that winter sees,
Will this thought rise on those who will meet my face no more,
  'He was one who had an eye for such mysteries'?

And will any say when my bell of quittance is heard in the
    gloom,
  And a crossing breeze cuts a pause in its outrollings,
Till they rise again, as they were a new bell's boom,
  'He hears it not now, but used to notice such things'?

CHRISTOPHER HASSALL

1912–64

Santa Claus
in a department store

Wolsey, or possibly my John of Gaunt,
Was the best thing I did. Come over here,
Behind the Christmas crib. (I'm not supposed
To let the children see me having tea.)
To tell the truth I'm glad of this engagement.
Dozens applied, but all they said was Thank you,
We'll stick to Mr Borthwick.
It's nice to feel one has given satisfaction.
Time was I had it all at my finger-tips,
Could plant a whisper in the back of the pit,
Or hold them breathless with the authority
Of absolute repose – a skill despised,
Not seen, in *your* day. It amounts to this:
Technique's no more than the bare bones. There are some
Unwittingly instil the faith that Man
Is greater than he knows. This I fell short of.
   You never met my wife. You are too young.
She often came with me on tour. One night
At Nottingham, got back from the show, and there
She was. I knew at once what made her do it.
She had resented me for years. No, not
Myself, but what she knew was *in* me, my
Belief in – Sir, forgive me if I say
My 'art', for I had shown, you'll understand,
Some promise. To use her word, she felt herself
'Usurped', and by degrees, unconsciously,
She managed somehow to diminish me,
Parch all my vital streams. A look would do it.
I was a kind of shrunken river-bed
Littered with tins, old tyres, and bicycle frames.

Well, that was years ago, and by then too late
To start afresh. Yet all the while I loved her.
Explain that if you can. . . . By all means, madam,
Those clocks are very popular this year.
I'll call the man in charge. No, there's no risk
Of damage. They pack the cuckoo separately.

ADRIAN HENRI
born 1932

I like this poem because I have loved Liverpool since I
lived near the Mersey at Bebington many years ago, and it
is a city which I continue to visit. There's a great vitality
about the place, maybe caused by the salt winds which
come up the river from the sea.

Mrs Albion You've Got a Lovely Daughter

For Allen Ginsberg

Albion's most lovely daughter sat on the banks of the
    Mersey dangling her landing stage in the water.

The daughters of Albion
    arriving by underground at Central Station
    eating hot ecclescakes at the Pierhead
    writing 'Billy Blake is fab' on a wall in Matthew St

    taking off their navyblue schooldrawers and
    putting on nylon panties ready for the night

The daughters of Albion
    see the moonlight beating down on them in Bebington
    throw away their chewinggum ready for the goodnight
        kiss
sleep in the dinnertime sunlight with old men
    looking up their skirts in St Johns Gardens
comb their darkblonde hair in suburban bedrooms
powder their delicate little nipples/wondering if tonight will
        be the night
their bodies pressed into dresses or sweaters
lavender at The Cavern or pink at The Sink

The daughters of Albion
        wondering how to explain why they didn't go home

The daughters of Albion
        taking the dawn ferry to tomorrow
        worrying about what happened
        worrying about what hasn't happened
        lacing up blue sneakers over brown ankles
        fastening up brown stockings to blue suspenderbelts

        Beautiful boys with bright red guitars
        in the spaces between the stars

        Reelin' an' a-rockin'
        Wishin' an' a-hopin'
        Kissin' an' a-prayin'
        Lovin' an' a-layin'

Mrs Albion you've got a lovely daughter.

QUINTIN HOGG
born 1907

Remembrance Day

Grieve not for these our dead. The evening star
By her own loveliness assurance gives
That beauty in a darkened world still lives;
So they to us their own sweet sureties are
That goodness still outshines the shades of war.
God is not mocked; his mercy still contrives
Peace for the bleeding flesh, the tired soul shrives
Pronouncing tranquil judgment from afar.
And these were his beloved; have no fear
For them, as, if in hardened hearts like ours
Love sprang unbidden for them, like the flowers
In those their English meadows, yet more dear
Must they remain to him whose gentle tear
Fell for this friend beneath proud Herod's Towers.

GERARD MANLEY HOPKINS
1845–89

Spring

Nothing is so beautiful as spring –
   When weeds, in wheels, shoot long and lovely and lush;
   Thrush's eggs look little low heavens, and thrush
Through the echoing timber does so rinse and wring
The ear, it strikes like lightnings to hear him sing;
   The glassy peartree leaves and blooms, they brush
   The descending blue; that blue is all in a rush
With richness; the racing lambs too have fair their fling.

What is all this juice and all this joy?
   A strain of the earth's sweet being in the beginning
     In Eden garden. – Have, get, before it cloy,
   Before it cloud, Christ, lord, and sour with sinning,
Innocent mind and Mayday in girl and boy,
   Most, O maid's child, thy choice and worthy the winning.

A. E. HOUSMAN
1860–1936

Into my heart

Into my heart an air that kills
   From yon far country blows:
What are those blue remembered hills,
   What spires, what farms are those?

That is the land of lost content,
   I see it shining plain,
The happy highways where I went
   And cannot come again.

GERARD IRVINE
born 1920

The Rev. Gerard Irvine, hard-working vicar of St Matthew's, Westminster, wrote this poem when he was at Oxford. It is reproduced from his collection *Sunset and Evening Star*.

The Death of Elizabeth Gaskell

'After leaving Manchester she went to stay at her attractive little house which was called the Lawn at Holybourne, near Alton in Hampshire. She had been to church (for her tenets did not prevent her from attending the services of a body not her own) and her son-in-law and daughters were seated at tea in the drawingroom, when she fell forward dead. This was on Sunday afternoon, November 12th, 1865' (from *Elizabeth Gaskell and Her Friends*, by Elizabeth Haldane).

Unlace your bonnet in the drawingroom,
    Late home from Church of England evensong,
Where limp late roses glint in Hampshire gloom,

And moist November breeze is borne along
    The stuccoed walls and lawns and bourne; and soon
Deep from the hall will sound the teatime gong,

And maids will draw the curtains. Macaroon
    Seedcake and muffin gleam where, warm and free,
The lamplight plays on sugartongs and spoon,

And mirrored in the pierglass grey eyes see
    The waxfruit, rosewood, Charlotte's[1] favourite chair,
Your son-in-law and daughters sipping tea.

[1]Charlotte Brontë

82

Tinkle of cup and saucer; crisp the air
      Outside, and mists from off the lawn arise.
But see: the phantom Stranger standing there

And beckoning you to follow; close your eyes,
      And, softly slumbering over Sunday tea,
Enter your unitarian paradise.

ELIZABETH JENNINGS

born 1926

Answers

I kept my answers small and kept them near;
Big questions bruised my mind but still I let
Small answers be a bulwark to my fear.

The huge abstractions I kept from the light;
Small things I handled and caressed and loved.
I let the stars assume the whole of night.

But the big answers clamoured to be moved
Into my life. Their great audacity
Shouted to be acknowledged and believed.

Even when all small answers build up to
Protection of my spirit, still I hear
Big answers striving for their overthrow

And all the great conclusions coming near.

LIONEL JOHNSON
1867–1902

The more things change, the more they remain the same!

Lambeth Lyric

Some seven score Bishops late at Lambeth sat,
Gray-whiskered and respectable debaters:
Each had on head a well-strung curly hat;
    And each wore gaiters.

And when these prelates at their talk had been
Long time, they made yet longer proclamation,
Saying: 'These creeds are childish! both Nicene,
    And Athanasian.

'True, they were written by the Holy Ghost;
So, to re-write them were perhaps a pity.
Refer we their revision to a most
    Select Committee!

'In ten years' time we wise Pan Anglicans
Once more around this Anglo Catholic table
Will meet, to prove God's word more weak than man's,
    His truth, less stable.'

So saying homeward the good Fathers go;
Up Mississippi some and some up Niger.
For thine old mantle they have clearly no
    More use, Elijah!

Instead, an apostolic apron girds
Their loins, which ministerial fingers tie on:
And Babylon's songs they sing, new tune and words,
    All over Zion.

The Creeds, the Scriptures, all the Faith of old,
They hack and hew to please each bumptious German,
Windy and vague as mists and clouds that fold
        Tabour and Hermon.

Happy Establishment in this thine hour!
Behold thy bishops to their sees retreating!
'Have at the Faith!' each cries: 'good bye till our
        Next merry meeting!'

JOHN KEATS
1795–1821

His Last Sonnet

Bright star! would I were steadfast as thou art –
  Not in lone splendour hung aloft the night,
And watching, with eternal lids apart,
  Like Nature's patient, sleepless Eremite,
The moving waters at their priestlike task
  Of pure ablution round earth's human shores,
Or gazing on the new soft fallen mask
  Of snow upon the mountains and the moors –
No – yet still steadfast, still unchangeable.
  Pillow'd upon my fair love's ripening breast,
To feel for ever its soft fall and swell,
  Awake for ever in a sweet unrest,
Still, still to hear her tender-taken breath,
And so live ever – or else swoon to death.

JOHN KEATS
1795–1821

From *The Eve of St Agnes*

I thought I would include both poems for St Agnes Eve
(Keats and Tennyson) as I like both, and this excerpt from
the Keats poem includes the particularly lovely lines:

> The arras, rich with horseman, hawk, and hound,
> Fluttered in the besieging wind's uproar;
> And the long carpets rose along the gusty floor.

XXXVIII

'My Madeline! sweet dreamer! lovely bride!
Say may I be for aye thy vassal blest?
Thy beauty's shield, heart-shaped and vermeil dyed?
Ah, silver shrine, here will I take my rest
After so many hours of toil and quest,
A famish'd pilgrim, – saved by miracle.
Though I have found, I will not rob thy nest
Saving of thy sweet self; if thou think'st well
To trust, fair Madeline, to no rude infidel.

XXXIX

'Hark! 'tis an elfin-storm from faery land,
Of haggard seeming, but a boon indeed:
Arise – arise! the morning is at hand; –
The bloated wassaillers will never heed: –
Let us away, my love, with happy speed;
There are no ears to hear, or eyes to see, –
Drown'd all in Rhenish and the sleepy mead:
Awake! arise! my love, and fearless be,
For o'er the southern moors I have a home for thee.'

XL

She hurried at his words, beset with fears,
For there were sleeping dragons all around,
At glaring watch, perhaps, with ready spears –
Down the wide stairs a darkling way they found. –
In all the house was heard no human sound.
A chain-droop'd lamp was flickering by each door;
The arras, rich with horseman, hawk, and hound,
Flutter'd in the besieging wind's uproar;
And the long carpets rose along the gusty floor.

XLI

They glide, like phantoms, into the wide hall;
Like phantoms, to the iron porch, they glide;
Where lay the Porter, in uneasy sprawl,
With a huge empty flagon by his side:
The wakeful bloodhound rose, and shook his hide,
But his sagacious eye an inmate owns:
By one, and one, the bolts full easy slide: –
The chains lie silent on the footworn stones; –
The key turns, and the door upon its hinges groans,

XLII

And they are gone: ay, ages long ago
These lovers fled away into the storm.
That night the Baron dreamt of many a woe,
And all his warrior-guests, with shade and form
Of witch, and demon, and large coffin-worm,
Were long be-nightmared. Angela the old
Died palsy-twitch'd, with meagre face deform;
The Beadsman, after thousand aves told,
For aye unsought for slept among his ashes cold.

RUDYARD KIPLING

1865–1936

The Way Through the Woods

They shut the road through the woods
Seventy years ago.
Weather and rain have undone it again,
And now you would never know
There was once a road through the woods
Before they planted the trees.
It is underneath the coppice and heath
And the thin anemones.
Only the keeper sees
That, where the ring-dove broods,
And the badgers roll at ease,
There was once a road through the woods.

Yet, if you enter the woods
Of a summer evening late,
When the night-air cools on the trout-ringed pools
Where the otter whistles his mate,
(They fear not men in the woods,
Because they see so few)
You will hear the beat of a horse's feet,
And the swish of a skirt in the dew,
Steadily cantering through
The misty solitudes,
As though they perfectly knew
The old lost road through the woods. . . .
But there is no road through the woods.

CHARLES LAMB
1775–1834

The Old Familiar Faces

I have had playmates, I have had companions,
In my days of childhood, in my joyful school-days,
All, all are gone, the old familiar faces.

I have been laughing, I have been carousing,
Drinking late, sitting late, with my bosom cronies,
All, all are gone, the old familiar faces.

I loved a love once, fairest among women:
Closed are her doors on me, I must not see her –
All, all are gone, the old familiar faces.

I have a friend, a kinder friend has no man;
Like an ingrate, I left my friend abruptly;
Left him, to muse on the old familiar faces.

Ghost-like I paced round the haunts of my childhood,
Earth seemed a desert I was bound to traverse,
Seeking to find the old familiar faces.

Friend of my bosom, thou more than a brother,
Why wert not thou born in my father's dwelling?
So might we talk of the old familiar faces –

How some they have died, and some they have left me,
And some are taken from me; all are departed;
All, all are gone, the old familiar faces.

ALUN LEWIS
1915–44

All Day it has Rained . . .

All day it has rained, and we on the edge of the moors
Have sprawled in our bell-tents, moody and dull as boors,
Groundsheets and blankets spread on the muddy ground
And from the first grey wakening we have found
No refuge from the skirmishing fine rain
And the wind that made the canvas heave and flap
And the taut wet guy-ropes ravel out and snap.
All day the rain has glided, wave and mist and dream,
Drenching the gorse and heather, a gossamer stream
Too light to stir the acorns that suddenly
Snatched from their cups by the wild south-westerly
Pattered against the tent and our upturned dreaming faces.
And we stretched out, unbuttoning our braces,
Smoking a Woodbine, darning dirty socks,
Reading the Sunday papers – I saw a fox
And mentioned it in the note I scribbled home; –
And we talked of girls, and dropping bombs on Rome,
And thought of the quiet dead and the loud celebrities
Exhorting us to slaughter, and the herded refugees;
– Yet thought softly, morosely of them, and as indifferently
As of ourselves or those whom we
For years have loved, and will again
Tomorrow maybe love; but now it is the rain
Possesses us entirely, the twilight and the rain.

And I can remember nothing dearer or more to my heart
Than the child I watched in the woods on Saturday
Shaking down burning chestnuts for the schoolyard's merry
    play,
Or the shaggy patient dog who followed me
By Sheet and Steep and up the wooded scree
To the Shoulder o' Mutton where Edward Thomas brooded
    long
On death and beauty – till a bullet stopped his song.

HENRY WADSWORTH LONGFELLOW
1807–82

I have always liked Longfellow's poems, particularly the two following ones. The phrase 'an old moustache' in 'The Children's Hour' used to puzzle me, but I have since learned that this was a name given to the veterans of Napoleon's army – 'The Old Moustaches'.

The Old Clock on the Stairs

> *L'éternité est une pendule, dont le balancier dit et redit sans cesse ces deux mots sentement, dans le silence des tombeaux; 'Toujours! jamais! Jamais! toujours!'*
>
> Jacques Bridaine

Somewhat back from the village street
Stands the old-fashioned country-seat.
Across its antique portico
Tall poplar-trees their shadows throw.
And from its station in the hall
An ancient timepiece says to all, –
      'Forever – never!
      Never – forever!'

Halfway up the stairs it stands,
And points and beckons with its hands
From its case of massive oak,
Like a monk, who, under his cloak,
Crosses himself, and sighs, alas!
With sorrowful voice to all who pass, –
      'Forever – never!
      Never – forever!'

By day its voice is low and light;
But in the silent dead of night,
Distinct as a passing footstep's fall,
It echoes along the vacant hall,
Along the ceiling, along the floor,
And seems to say, at each chamber door, –
      'Forever – never!
      Never – forever!'

Through days of sorrow and of mirth,
Through days of death and days of birth,
Through every swift vicissitude
Of changeful time, unchanged it has stood,
And as if, like God, it all things saw,
It calmly repeats those words of awe, –
      'Forever – never!
      Never – forever!'

In that mansion used to be
Free-hearted Hospitality;
His great fires up the chimney roared;
The stranger feasted at his board;
But, like the skeleton at the feast,
That warning timepiece never ceased, –
      'Forever – never!
      Never – forever!'

There groups of merry children played,
There youth and maidens dreaming strayed;
O precious hours! O golden prime,
And affluence of love and time!
Even as a miser counts his gold,
Those hours the ancient timepiece told, –
      'Forever – never!
      Never – forever!'

From that chamber, clothed in white,
The bride came forth on her wedding night;
There, in that silent room below,
The dead lay in his shroud of snow;
And in the hush that followed the prayer,
Was heard the old clock on the stair, –
　　　'Forever – never!
　　　Never – forever!'

All are scattered now and fled,
Some are married, some are dead;
And when I ask, with throbs of pain,
'Ah! when shall they all meet again?'
As in the days long since gone by,
The ancient timepiece makes reply, –
　　　'Forever – never!
　　　Never – forever!'

Never here, forever there,
Where all parting, pain, and care,
And death, and time shall disappear, –
Forever there, but never here!
The horologe of Eternity
Sayeth this incessantly, –
　　　'Forever – never!
　　　Never – forever!'

HENRY WADSWORTH LONGFELLOW
1807–82

The Children's Hour

Between the dark and the daylight
 When the night is beginning to lower,
Comes a pause in the day's occupations,
That is known as the Children's Hour.

I hear in the chamber above me
 The patter of little feet,
The sound of a door that is opened,
 And voices soft and sweet.

From my study I see in the lamp-light,
 Descending the broad hall stair,
Grave Alice, and laughing Allegra,
 And Edith with golden hair.

A whisper, and then a silence:
 Yet I know by their merry eyes
They are plotting and planning together
 To take me by surprise.

A sudden rush from the stairway,
 A sudden raid from the hall!
By three doors left unguarded
 They enter my castle wall!

They climb up into my turret
 O'er the arms and back of my chair;
If I try to escape, they surround me;
 They seem to be everywhere.

They almost devour me with kisses,
 Their arms about me entwine,
Till I think of the Bishop of Bingen
 In his Mouse-Tower on the Rhine!

Do you think, O blue-eyed banditti,
    Because you have scaled the wall
Such an old moustache as I am
    Is not a match for you all!

I have you fast in my fortress,
    And will not let you depart,
But put you down into the dungeon
    In the round-tower of my heart.

And there will I keep you for ever,
    Yes, for ever and a day,
Till the walls shall crumble to ruin,
    And moulder in dust away!

ROSE MACAULAY

1881–1958

The Devourers

Cambridge town is a beleaguered city;
   For south and north, like a sea,
Are beat on its gates, without haste or pity,
   The downs and the fen country.

Cambridge towers, so old, so wise,
   They were builded but yesterday,
Watched by sleepy gray secret eyes
   That smiled as at children's play.

Roads south of Cambridge run into the waste,
   Where learning and lamps are not,
And the pale downs tumble, blind, chalk-faced,
   And the brooding churches squat.

Roads north of Cambridge march through a plain
   Level like the traitor sea.
It will swallow its ships, and turn and smile again –
   The insatiable fen country.

Lest the downs and the fens should eat Cambridge up,
   And its towers be tossed and thrown,
And its rich wine drunk from its broken cup,
   And its beauty no more known –

Let us come, you and I, where the roads run blind,
   Out beyond the transient city,
That our love, mingling with earth, may find
   Her imperishable heart of pity.

HUGH MACDIARMID
1892–1978

The Two Parents

I love my little son, and yet when he was ill
I could not confine myself to his bedside.
I was impatient of his squalid little needs,
His laboured breathing and the fretful way he cried
And longed for my wide range of interests again,
Whereas his mother sank without another care
To that dread level of nothing but life itself
And stayed day and night, till he was better, there.

Women may pretend, yet they always dismiss
Everything but mere being just like this.

ANDREW MARVELL

1621–78

The Mower to the Glo-Worms

I

Ye living Lamps, by whose dear light
The Nightingale does sit so late,
And studying all the Summer-night,
Her matchless Songs does meditate;

II

Ye Country Comets, that portend
No War, nor Prince's funeral,
Shining unto no higher end
Then to presage the Grasses fall;

III

Ye Glo-worms, whose officious Flame
To wandring Mowers shows the way,
That in the Night have lost their aim,
And after foolish Fires do stray;

IV

Your courteous Lights in vain you wast,
Since *Juliana* here is come,
For She my Mind hath so displac'd
That I shall never find my home.

JOHN MASEFIELD
1896–1967

Twilight

Twilight it is, and the far woods are dim, and the rooks
       cry and call.
Down in the valley the lamps, and the mist, and a star over all,
There by the rick, where they thresh, is the drone at an end,
Twilight it is, and I travel the road with my friend.

I think of the friends who are dead, who were dear long ago
       in the past,
Beautiful friends who are dead, though I know that death
       cannot last;
Friends with the beautiful eyes that the dust has defiled,
Beautiful souls who were gentle when I was a child.

GEORGE MATHESON
1842–1906

Gather us in

I always liked this hymn, which was in the Congregational Hymnary when I was a child. Although the names of some of the countries mentioned have changed, the subject is up-to-date in these ecumenical days. The hymn disappeared from the hymnary some years ago, and when I asked about it I was told that it was 'theologically unsound'. Well, I'm no theologian, and I still like it.

Them also I must bring, and they shall hear My voice,

Gather us in, Thou Love that fillest all!
  Gather our rival faiths within Thy fold!
Rend each man's temple-veil and bid it fall,
    That we may know that Thou has been of old;
      Gather us in.

Gather us in: we worship only Thee:
  In varied names we stretch a common hand;
In diverse forms a common soul we see;
    In many ships we seek one spirit-land;
      Gather us in.

Each sees one colour of Thy rainbow-light,
  Each looks upon one tint and calls it heaven;
Thou art the fulness of our partial sight;
    We are not perfect till we find the seven;
      Gather us in.

Thine is the mystic life great India craves,
  Thine is the Parsee's sin-destroying beam,
Thine is the Buddhist's rest from tossing waves,
    Thine is the empire of vast China's dream;
      Gather us in.

Thine is the Roman's strength without his pride,
    Thine is the Greek's glad world without its graves,
Thine is Judæa's law with love beside,
    The truth that censures and the grace that saves;
            Gather us in.

Some seek a Father in the heavens above,
    Some ask a human image to adore,
Some crave a spirit vast as life and love:
    Within Thy mansions we have all and more;
            Gather us in.

JOHN McCRAE
1827–1918

In Flanders Fields

I have included this poem, although it is very well
known, because it reminds me of the ease with which one
can know a poem by heart without really listening to it
thoroughly. Only recently I suddenly realized that the
last two lines refer to the soporific effect of the poppies.

In Flanders fields the poppies blow
Between the crosses, row on row
   That mark our place; and in the sky
   The larks, still bravely singing, fly
Scarce heard amid the guns below.

We are the Dead. Short days ago
We lived, felt dawn, saw sunset glow,
   Loved and were loved, and now we lie
     In Flanders fields.

Take up our quarrel with the foe:
To you from failing hands we throw
   The torch; be yours to hold it high.
   If ye break faith with us who die
We shall not sleep, though poppies grow
     In Flanders fields.

WILLIAM McGONAGALL
1830–1902

I had to include William McGonagall – who couldn't like him? – for his unconscious humour, his pathos and his bathos!

Descriptive Jottings of London

As I stood upon London Bridge and viewed the mighty throng
Of thousands of people in cabs and 'busses rapidly whirling along,
All furiously driving to and fro,
Up one street and down another as quick as they could go:

Then I was struck with the discordant sounds of human voices there,
Which seemed to me like wild geese cackling in the air:
And the river Thames is a most beautiful sight,
To see the steamers sailing upon it by day and by night.

And the Tower of London is most gloomy to behold,
And the crown of England lies there, begemmed with precious stones and gold;
King Henry the Sixth was murdered there by the Duke of Glo'ster,
And when he killed him with his sword he called him an impostor.

St Paul's Cathedral is the finest building that ever I did see,
There's no building can surpass it in the city of Dundee,
Because it's magnificent to behold,
With its beautiful dome and spire glittering like gold.

And as for Nelson's Monument that stands in Trafalgar
    Square,
It is a most stately monument I most solemnly declare,
And towering defiantly very high,
Which arrests strangers' attention while passing by.

Then there's two beautiful water-fountains spouting up very
    high,
Where the weary traveller can drink when he feels dry;
And at the foot of the monument there's three bronze lions
    in grand array,
Enough to make the stranger's heart throb with dismay.

Then there's Mr Spurgeon, a great preacher, which no one
    dare gainsay,
I went to hear him preach on the Sabbath-day,
And he made my heart feel light and gay,
When I heard him preach and pray.

And the Tabernacle was crowded from ceiling to floor,
And many were standing outside the door;
He is an eloquent preacher I honestly declare,
And I was struck with admiration as on him I did stare.

Then there's Petticoat Lane I venture to say,
It's a wonderful place on the Sabbath-day;
There wearing apparel can be bought to suit the young or old,
For the ready cash, silver, coppers, or gold.

Oh! mighty city of London! you are wonderful to see,
And thy beauties no doubt fill the tourist's heart with glee;
But during my short stay, and while wandering there,
Mr Spurgeon was the only man I heard speaking proper
    English I do declare.

WILLIAM McGONAGALL
1830–1902

The Royal Review:
25 August 1881

All hail to the Empress of India, Great Britain's Queen –
Long may she live in health, happy and serene –
That came from London, far away,
To review the Scottish Volunteers in grand array:
Most magnificent to be seen,
Near by Salisbury Crags and its pastures green,
Which will long be remembered by our gracious Queen –

And by the Volunteers, that came from far away,
Because it rain'd most of the day.
And with the rain their clothes were wet all through,
On the 25th day of August, at the Royal Review.
And to the Volunteers it was no lark,
Because they were ankle deep in mud in the Queen's Park,
Which proved to the Queen they were loyal and true,
To endure such hardships at the Royal Review.

Oh! it was a most beautiful scene
To see the Forfarshire Artillery marching past the Queen;
Her Majesty with their steady marching felt content,
Especially when their arms to her they did present.

And the Inverness Highland Volunteers seemed verygran',
And marched by steady to a man
Amongst the mud without dismay,
And the rain pouring down on them all the way.
And the bands they did play, God Save the Queen,
Near by Holyrood Palace and the Queen's Park so green.

Success to our noble Scottish Volunteers!
I hope they will be spared for many long years,
And to Her Majesty always prove loyal and true,
As they have done for the second time at the Royal Review.

To take them in general, they behaved very well,
The more that the rain fell on them pell-mell.
They marched by Her Majesty in very grand array,
Which will be remembered for many a long day,
Bidding defiance to wind and rain,
Which adds the more fame to their name.

And I hope none of them will have cause to rue
The day that they went to the Royal Review.
And I'm sure Her Majesty ought to feel proud,
And in her praise she cannot speak too loud,
Because the more that it did rain they did not mourn,
Which caused Her Majesty's heart with joy to burn,
Because she knew they were loyal and true
For enduring such hardships at the Royal Review.

ALICE MEYNELL

1847–1922

Renouncement

I must not think of thee; and, tired yet strong,
I shun the thought that lurks in all delight –
The thought of thee – and in the blue Heaven's height,
And in the sweetest passage of a song.
Oh, just beyond the fairest thoughts that throng
This breast, the thought of thee waits, hidden yet bright;
But it must never, never come in sight;
I must stop short of thee the whole day long.

But when sleep comes to close each difficult day,
When night gives pause to the long watch I keep,
And all my bonds I needs must lose apart,
Must doff my will as raiment laid away, –
With the first dream that comes with the first sleep
I run, I run, I am gathered to thy heart.

CAROLINE NORTON
1808–76

I do not love thee

I do not love thee! – no! I do not love thee!
And yet when thou art absent I am sad;
   And envy even the bright blue sky above thee,
Whose quiet stars may see thee and be glad.

I do not love thee! – yet, I know not why,
Whate'er thou dost seems still well done, to me:
   And often in my solitude I sigh
That those I do love are not more like thee!

   I do not love thee! – yet, when thou art gone,
I hate the sound (though those who speak be dear)
   Which breaks the lingering echo of the tone
Thy voice of music leaves upon my ear.

   I do not love thee! – yet thy speaking eyes,
With their deep, bright, and most expressive blue,
   Between me and the midnight heaven arise,
Oftener than any eyes I ever knew.

   I know I do not love thee! yet, alas!
Others will scarcely trust my candid heart;
   And oft I catch them smiling as they pass,
Because they see me gazing where thou art.

WILFRED OWEN
1893–1918

Strange Meeting

It seemed that out of battle I escaped
Down some profound dull tunnel, long since scooped
Through granites which titanic wars had groined.
Yet also there encumbered sleepers groaned,
Too fast in thought or death to be bestirred.
Then, as I probed them, one sprang up, and stared
With piteous recognition in fixed eyes,
Lifting distressful hands as if to bless.
And by his smile, I knew that sullen hall,
By his dead smile I knew we stood in Hell.
With a thousand pains that vision's face was gained;
Yet no blood reached there from the upper ground,
And no guns thumped, or down the flues made moan.
'Strange friend,' I said, 'here is no cause to mourn.'
'None,' said the other, 'save the undone years,
The hopelessness. Whatever hope is yours,
Was my life also; I went hunting wild
After the wildest beauty in the world,
Which lies not calm in eyes, or braided hair,
But mocks the steady running of the hour,
And if it grieves, grieves richlier than here.
For by my glee might many men have laughed,
And of my weeping something had been left,
Which must die now. I mean the truth untold,
The pity of war, the pity war distilled.
Now men will go content with what we spoiled.
Or, discontent, boil bloody, and be spilled.
They will be swift with swiftness of the tigress,
None will break ranks, though nations trek from progress.
Courage was mine, and I had mystery,
Wisdom was mine, and I had mastery;
To miss the march of this retreating world
Into vain citadels that are not walled.

Then, when much blood had clogged their chariot-wheels
I would go up and wash them from sweet wells,
Even with truths that lie too deep for taint.
I would have poured my spirit without stint
But not through wounds; not on the cess of war.
Foreheads of men have bled where no wounds were.
I am the enemy you killed, my friend.
I knew you in this dark; for so you frowned
Yesterday through me as you jabbed and killed.
I parried; but my hands were loath and cold.
Let us sleep now. . . .'

EDGAR ALLAN POE
1809–49

The Raven

Some readers may think Poe's writings too melodramatic for their taste, although this side of his nature is not evident in the gentle melancholy of 'Annabel Lee'. I find 'The Raven' interesting technically, as well as for its content. In his essay 'The Philosophy of Composition' Poe describes how he built up the plan of the poem step by step, starting with the simple word 'Nevermore'. He then cast about for some 'Non-thinking creature' to repeat the word, and after discarding the idea of a parrot, decided upon a raven. The theme was to be a melancholy one – that of death.

> 'When' I said, 'is this most melancholy of topics most poetical? When it most closely allies itself to Beauty; the death then, of a beautiful woman is unquestionably the most poetical topic in the world, and equally it is beyond doubt that the lips best suited for such topics are those of a bereaved lover.'

Having then devised the plan of a question and answer, he at last put pen to paper, and wrote the *final* stanza, to establish the climax.

Poe uses an unusual structure for 'The Raven' – a double rhyme in the first and third lines, each stanza consisting of five lines; the second, fourth and fifth lines rhyme, and then the refrain incorporates the word 'Nevermore'. All this was carefully planned and the whole effect is thrilling and dramatic.

The volume of Poe's *Selected Poems* from which I took the notes is dedicated to Elizabeth Barrett (Browning), and illustrated by W. Heath Robinson before the days of his more famous inventions and comic drawings.

Once upon a midnight dreary, while I pondered,
      weak and weary,
Over many a quaint and curious volume of forgotten
      lore –
While I nodded, nearly napping, suddenly there came
      a tapping,
As of some one gently rapping – rapping at my
      chamber door.
' 'Tis some visitor,' I muttered, 'tapping at my
      chamber door –
    Only this and nothing more.'
Ah, distinctly I remember, it was in the bleak
      December,
And each separate dying ember wrought its ghost
      upon the floor.
Eagerly I wished the morrow; – vainly I had sought
      to borrow
From my books surcease of sorrow – sorrow for the
      lost Lenore –
For the rare and radiant maiden whom the angels
      name Lenore –
    Nameless here for evermore.

And the silken sad uncertain rustling of each purple
      curtain
Thrilled me – filled me with fantastic terrors never
      felt before;
So that now, to still the beating of my heart, I stood
      repeating
'Tis some visitor entreating entrance at my chamber
      door –
Some late visitor entreating entrance at my chamber
      door; –
    This it is and nothing more.'
Presently my soul grew stronger; hesitating then no
      longer,
'Sir,' said I, 'or Madam, truly your forgiveness I
      implore;
But the fact is I was napping, and so gently you came
      rapping,

And so faintly you came tapping – tapping at my
    chamber door,
That I scarce was sure I heard you' – here I opened
    wide the door: –
      Darkness there and nothing more.

Deep into that darkness peering, long I stood there
    wondering, fearing,
Doubting, dreaming dreams no mortal ever dared to
    dream before;
But the silence was unbroken, and the darkness gave
    no token,
And the only word there spoken was the whispered
    word, 'Lenore!'
This I whispered, and an echo murmured back the
    word, 'Lenore!'
      Merely this and nothing more.

Back into the chamber turning, all my soul within me
    burning,
Soon I heard again a tapping, somewhat louder than
    before.
'Surely,' said I, 'surely that is something at my
    window lattice;
Let me see, then, what thereat is, and this mystery
    explore –
Let my heart be still a moment, and this mystery
    explore; –
      'Tis the wind and nothing more.'

Open here I flung the shutter, when, with many a flirt
    and flutter,
In there stepped a stately Raven of the saintly days
    of yore;
Not the least obeisance made he; not an instant
    stopped or stayed he;
But, with mien of lord or lady, perched above my
    chamber door –

Perched upon a bust of Pallas just above my chamber
        door –
    Perched, and sat, and nothing more

Then this ebony bird beguiling my sad fancy into
        smiling,
By the grave and stern decorum of the countenance it
        wore,
'Though thy crest be shorn and shaven, thou,' I said,
    'art sure no craven,
Ghastly grim and ancient Raven wandering from the
        Nightly shore –
Tell me what thy lordly name is on the Night's
        Plutonian shore!'
    Quoth the Raven, 'Nevermore.'

Much I marvelled this ungainly fowl to hear discourse
        so plainly,
Though its answer little meaning – little relevancy
        bore;
For we cannot help agreeing that no living human
        being
Ever yet was blessed with seeing bird above his
        chamber door –
Bird or beast upon the sculptured bust above his
        chamber door,
    With such name as 'Nevermore.'

But the Raven, sitting lonely on that placid bust,
        spoke only
That one word, as if his soul in that one word he did
        outpour.
Nothing further then he uttered – not a feather then
        he fluttered –
Till I scarcely more than muttered, 'Other friends
        have flown before –
On the morrow *he* will leave me, as my hopes have
        flown before.'
    Then the bird said, 'Nevermore.'

Startled at the stillness broken by reply so aptly
        spoken,
'Doubtless,' said I, 'what it utters is its only stock
        and store,
Caught from some unhappy master whom unmerciful
        Disaster
Followed fast and followed faster till his songs one
        burden bore –
Till the dirges of his Hope the melancholy burden
        bore
    Of "Never – nevermore." '

But the Raven still beguiling all my sad soul into
        smiling,
Straight I wheeled a cushioned seat in front of bird
        and bust and door;
Then, upon the velvet sinking, I betook myself to
        linking
Fancy unto fancy, thinking what this ominous bird of
        yore –
What this grim, ungainly, ghastly, gaunt, and ominous
        bird of yore
    Meant in croaking 'Nevermore.'

This I sat engaged in guessing, but no syllable
        expressing
To the fowl whose fiery eyes now burned into my
        bosom's core;
This and more I sat divining, with my head at ease
        reclining
On the cushion's velvet lining that the lamp-light
        gloated o'er,
But whose velvet violet lining with the lamp-light
        gloating o'er,
    She shall press, ah, nevermore!

Then, methought, the air grew denser, perfumed from
        an unseen censer
Swung by Seraphim whose foot-falls tinkled on the
        tufted floor.

'Wretch,' I cried, 'thy God hath lent thee – by these
    angels he hath sent thee
Respite – respite and nepenthe from thy memories of
    Lenore!
Quaff, oh quaff this kind nepenthe, and forget this
    lost Lenore!'
    Quoth the Raven, 'Nevermore.'

'Prophet!' said I, 'thing of evil! – prophet still, if
    bird or devil! –
Whether Tempter sent, or whether tempest tossed
    thee here ashore,
Desolate yet all undaunted, on this desert land
    enchanted –
On this home by Horror haunted – tell me truly, I
    implore –
Is there – *is* there balm in Gilead? – tell me – tell me,
    I implore!'
    Quoth the Raven, 'Nevermore.'

'Prophet!' said I, 'thing of evil! – prophet still, if
    bird or devil!
By that Heaven that bends above us – by that God
    we both adore –
Tell this soul with sorrow laden if, within the distant
    Aidenn,
It shall clasp a sainted maiden whom the angels name
    Lenore –
Clasp a rare and radiant maiden whom the angels
    name Lenore.'
    Quoth the Raven, 'Nevermore.'

'Be that word our sign of parting, bird or fiend!' I
    shrieked, upstarting –
'Get thee back into the tempest and the Night's
    Plutonian shore!
Leave no black plume as a token of that lie thy soul
    hath spoken!

118

Leave my loneliness unbroken! – quit the bust above
      my door!
Take thy beak from out my heart, and take thy form
      from off my door!'
    Quoth the Raven, 'Nevermore.'

And the Raven, never flitting, still is sitting, still is
      sitting
On the pallid bust of Pallas just above my chamber
      door;
And his eyes have all the seeming of a demon's that
      is dreaming,
And the lamp-light o'er him streaming throws his
      shadow on the floor;
And my soul from out that shadow that lies floating
      on the floor
    Shall be lifted – nevermore!

ARTHUR QUILLER-COUCH
1863–1944

Alma Mater

Know you her secret none can utter?
   Hers of the Book, the tripled Crown?
Still on the spire the pigeons flutter,
   Still by the gateway flits the gown;
Still on the street, from corbel and gutter,
   Faces of stone look down.

Faces of stone, and stonier faces –
   Some from library windows wan
Forth on her gardens, her green spaces,
   Peer and turn to their books anon.
Hence, my Muse, from the green oases
   Gather the tent, begone!

Nay, should she by the pavement linger
   Under the rooms where once she played,
Who from the feast would rise to fling her
   One poor *sou* for her serenade?
One short laugh for the antic finger
   Thrumming a lute-string frayed?

Once, my dear – but the world was young then –
   Magdalen elms and Trinity limes –
Lissom the blades and the backs that swung then,
   Eight good men in the good old times –
Careless we, and the chorus flung then
   Under St Mary's chimes!

Reins lay loose and the ways led random –
   Christ Church meadow and Iffley track,
'Idleness horrid and dog-cart' (tandem),
   Aylesbury grind and Bicester pack –
Pleasant our lines, and faith! we scanned 'em;
   Having that artless knack.

Come, old limmer, the times grow colder;
    Leaves of the creeper redden and fall.
Was it a hand then clapped my shoulder? –
    Only the wind by the chapel wall!
Dead leaves drift on the lute . . . So fold her
    Under the faded shawl.

Never we wince, though none deplore us,
    We who go reaping that we sowed;
Cities at cockcrow wake before us –
    Hey, for the lilt of the London road!
One look back, and a rousing chorus!
    Never a palinode!

Still on her spire the pigeons hover;
    Still by her gateway haunts the gown.
Ah, but her secret? You, young lover,
    Drumming her old ones forth from town,
Know you the secret none discover?
    Tell it – when *you* go down.

Yet if at length you seek her, prove her,
    Lean to her whispers never so nigh;
Yet if at last not less her lover
    You in your hansom leave the High;
Down from her towers a ray shall hover –
    Touch you, a passer-by.

KATHLEEN RAINE
born 1908

Envoi

Take of me what is not my own,
my love, my beauty, and my poem –
the pain is mine, and mine alone.

See how against the weight in the bone
the hawk hangs perfect in mid-air –
the blood pays dear to raise it there,
the moment, not the bird, divine.

And see the peaceful trees extend
their myriad leaves in leisured dance –
they bear the weight of sky and cloud
upon the fountain of their veins.

In rose with petals soft as air
I bind for you the tides and fire –
the death that lives within the flower,
oh gladly, love, for you I bear!

RAINER MARIA RILKE
1875–1926

Joseph's Suspicion

And the angel, taking some pains, told
Considerately the man who clenched his fists:
'But can't you see in her robe's every fold
That she is cool as the Lord's morning mists?'

But the other murmured, looking sinister:
'What is it that has wrought this change in her?'
Then cried the angel to him: 'Carpenter,
Can't you see yet that God is acting here?'

'Because you plane the planks, of your pride could
You really make the Lord God answerable,
Who unpretentiously from the same wood
Makes the leaves burst forth, the young buds swell?'

He understood that. And then as he raised
His frightened glance towards the angel who
Had gone away . . . slowly the man drew
Off his heavy cap. Then in song he praised.

Translated from the German by C. F. MacIntyre

CHRISTINA ROSSETTI
1830–94

Maude Clare

Out of the church she followed them
    With a lofty step and mien:
His bride was like a village maid,
    Maude Clare was like a queen.

'Son Thomas,' his lady mother said,
    With smiles, almost with tears:
'May Nell and you but live as true
    As we have done for years;

'Your father thirty years ago
    Had just your tale to tell;
But he was not so pale as you,
    Nor I so pale as Nell.'

My lord was pale with inward strife,
    And Nell was pale with pride;
My lord gazed long on pale Maude Clare
    Or ever he kissed the bride.

'Lo, I have brought my gift, my lord,
    Have brought my gift,' she said:
'To bless the hearth, to bless the board,
    To bless the marriage-bed.

'Here's my half of the golden chain
    You wore about your neck,
That day we waded ankle-deep
    For lilies in the beck:

'Here's my half of the faded leaves
    We plucked from budding bough,
With feet amongst the lily leaves, –
    The lilies are budding now.'

He strove to match her scorn with scorn,
    He faltered in his place:
'Lady,' he said, – 'Maude Clare,' he said, –
    'Maude Clare,' – and hid his face.

She turn'd to Nell: 'My Lady Nell,
    I have a gift for you;
Though, were it fruit, the blooms were gone,
    Or, were it flowers, the dew.

'Take my share of a fickle heart,
    Mine of a paltry love:
Take it or leave it as you will,
    I wash my hands thereof.'

'And what you leave,' said Nell, 'I'll take,
    And what you spurn, I'll wear;
For he's my lord for better and worse,
    And him I love, Maude Clare.

'Yea, though you're taller by the head,
    More wise and much more fair:
I'll love him till he loves me best,
    Me best of all, Maude Clare.'

SIEGFRIED SASSOON
1886–1967

At the Grave of Henry Vaughan

Henry Vaughan's poem 'Peace' follows later in this book.

Above the voiceful windings of a river
An old green slab of simply graven stone
Shuns notice, overshadowed by a yew.
Here Vaughan lies dead, whose name flows on for ever
Through pastures of the spirit washed with dew
And starlit with eternities unknown.

Here sleeps the Silurist; the loved physician;
The face that left no portraiture behind;
The skull that housed white angels and had vision
Of daybreak through the gateways of the mind.
    Here faith and mercy, wisdom and humility
    (Whose influence shall prevail for evermore)
   Shine. And this lowly grave tells Heaven's
     tranquillity . . .
    And here stand I, a suppliant at the door.

WILLIAM SHAKESPEARE
1564–1616

Suns and Clouds

Full many a glorious morning have I seen
Flatter the mountain-tops with sovereign eye,
Kissing with golden face the meadows green,
Gilding pale streams with heavenly alchemy;
Anon permit the basest clouds to ride
With ugly rack on his celestial face,
And from the forlorn world his visage hide,
Stealing unseen to west with this disgrace.

Even so my sun one early morn did shine
With all-triumphant splendour on my brow;
But out, alack! he was but one hour mine,
The region cloud hath masked him from me now.
Yet him for this my love no whit disdaineth;
Suns of the world may stain when heaven's sun staineth.

PERCY BYSSHE SHELLEY
1792–1822

From *Adonais*

An Elegy on the Death of John Keats

Peace, peace! he is not dead, he doth not sleep –
He hath awakened from the dream of life –
'Tis we, who lost in stormy visions, keep
With phantoms an unprofitable strife,
And in mad trance, strike with our spirit's knife
Invulnerable nothings. – *We* decay
Like corpses in a charnel; fear and grief
Convulse us and consume us day by day,
And cold hopes swarm like worms within our living clay.

He has outsoared the shadow of our night;
Envy and calumny and hate and pain,
And that unrest which men miscall delight,
Can touch him not and torture not again;
From the contagion of the world's slow stain
He is secure, and now can never mourn
A heart grown cold, a head grown gray in vain;
Nor, when the spirit's self has ceased to burn,
With sparkless ashes load an unlamented urn.

He lives, he wakes – 'tis Death is dead, not he;
Mourn not for Adonais. – Thou young Dawn
Turn all thy dew to splendour, for from thee
The spirit thou lamentest is not gone;
Ye caverns and ye forests, cease to moan!
Cease ye faint flowers and fountains, and thou Air,
Which like a mourning veil thy scarf hadst thrown
O'er the abandoned Earth, now leave it bare
Even to the joyous stars which smile on its despair!

He is made one with Nature: there is heard
His voice in all her music, from the moan
Of thunder, to the song of night's sweet bird;
He is a presence to be felt and known
In darkness and in light, from herb and stone,
Spreading itself where'er that Power may move
Which has withdrawn his being to its own;
Which wields the world with never wearied love,
Sustains it from beneath, and kindles it above.

JAMES SHIRLEY
1596–1666

Death the Leveller

I remember back in the 1960s a young man from a Liverpool paper came to interview me. He asked me the routine question, 'Don't you find it exciting and interesting to be in the centre of all these great doings?' and I replied by quoting the first verse of this poem. Poor young man – he was nonplussed. I was sorry afterwards, and it taught me not to be whimsical.

The glories of our blood and state
    Are shadows, not substantial things;
There is no armour against fate;
    Death lays his icy hand on kings:
        Sceptre and Crown
        Must tumble down,
And in the dust be equal made
With the poor crooked scythe and spade.

Some men with swords may reap the field,
    And plant fresh laurels where they kill:
But their strong nerves at last must yield;
    They tame but one another still:
        Early or late
        They stoop to fate,
And must give up their murmuring breath
When they, pale captives, creep to death.

The garlands wither on your brow;
    Then boast no more your mighty deeds;
Upon Death's purple altar now
    See where the victor-victim bleeds:
        Your heads must come
        To the cold tomb;
Only the actions of the just
Smell sweet, and blossom in their dust.

EDITH SITWELL

1887–1964

Still Falls the Rain

The raids, 1940. Night and Dawn

> The sub-title indicates that the poet is describing the rain
> of bombs in the Blitz.

Still falls the Rain –
Dark as the world of man, black as our loss –
Blind as the nineteen hundred and forty nails
Upon the Cross.

Still falls the Rain
With a sound like the pulse of the heart that is changed to the
     hammer-beat
In the Potter's Field, and the sound of the impious feet

On the Tomb:
               Still falls the Rain
In the Field of Blood where the small hopes breed and the
     human brain
Nurtures its greed, that worm with the brow of Cain.

Still falls the Rain
At the feet of the Starved Man hung upon the Cross.
Christ that each day, each night, nails there, have mercy on
     us –
On Dives and on Lazarus:
Under the Rain the sore and the gold are as one.

Still falls the Rain –
Still falls the Blood from the Starved Man's wounded Side:
He bears in His Heart all wounds, – those of the light that died,

131

The last faint spark
In the self-murdered heart, the wounds of the sad
    uncomprehending dark.
The wounds of the baited bear, –
The blind and weeping bear whom the keepers beat
On his helpless flesh . . . the tears of the hunted hare.

Still falls the Rain –
Then – O Ile leape up to my God: who pulles me doune –
See, see where Christ's blood streames in the firmament:
It flows from the Brow we nailed upon the tree
Deep to the dying, to the thirsting heart
That holds the fires of the world, – dark-smirched with pain
As Caesar's laurel crown.

Then sounds the voice of One who like the heart of man
  Was once a child who among beasts has lain –
'Still do I love, still shed my innocent light, my Blood, for thee.'

ALFRED, LORD TENNYSON
1809–92

From *Maud*

If one must choose a favourite poet, I would choose Tennyson, mainly perhaps because he is a country poet and his detailed descriptions of rural life bring back an echo of the remote village of my childhood. There are still pockets of true country left in England, but they are rare and hard to find.

I should have liked to include the whole of 'Maud' if there had been room; this poem or story, which was one of Tennyson's own favourites, is often only remembered now by one ballad, but 'Maud' is a highly dramatic tale of financial ruin, suicide, love, murder and remorse. In it we find the Victorian village with its wicked squire, its Hamlet-like hero, the squire's lovely daughter, and her foppish suitor. As a background to the story are beautifully detailed descriptions of the English countryside:

IV

I

A million emeralds break from the ruby-budded lime
In the little grove where I sit – ah, wherefore cannot I be
Like things of the season gay, like the bountiful season bland,
When the far-off sail is blown by the breeze of a softer clime,
Half-lost in the liquid azure bloom of a crescent of sea,
The silent sapphire-spangled marriage ring of the land?

II

Below me, there, is the village, and looks how quiet and small!
And yet bubbles o'er like a city, with gossip, scandal, and
    spite;
And Jack on his ale-house bench has as many lies as a Czar;
And here on the landward side, by a red rock, glimmers the
    Hall;
And up in the high Hall-garden I see her pass like a light;
But sorrow seize me if ever that light be my leading star!

III

When have I bow'd to her father, the wrinkled head of the
    race?
I met her to-day with her brother, but not to her brother I
    bow'd;
I bow'd to his lady-sister as she rode by on the moor;
But the fire of a foolish pride flash'd over her beautiful face.
O child, you wrong your beauty, believe it, in being so proud;
Your father has wealth well-gotten, and I am nameless and
    poor.

IV

I keep but a man and a maid, ever ready to slander and steal;
I know it, and smile a hard-set smile, like a stoic, or like
A wiser epicurean, and let the world have its way:
For nature is one with rapine, a harm no preacher can heal;
The Mayfly is torn by the swallow, the sparrow spear'd by the
    shrike,
And the whole little wood where I sit is a world of plunder and
    prey.

V

We are puppets, Man in his pride, and Beauty fair in her
    flower;
Do we move ourselves, or are moved by an unseen hand at a
    game
That pushes us off from the board, and others ever succeed?
Ah yet, we cannot be kind to each other here for an hour;
We whisper, and hint, and chuckle, and grin at a brother's
    shame;
However we brave it out, we men are a little breed.

VI

A monstrous eft was of old the Lord and Master of Earth,
For him did his high sun flame, and his river billowing ran,
And he felt himself in his force to be Nature's crowning race.
As nine months go to the shaping an infant ripe for his birth,
So many a million of ages have gone to the making of man:
He now is first, but is he the last? is he not too base?

VII

The man of science himself is fonder of glory, and vain,
An eye well-practised in nature, a spirit bounded and poor;
The passionate heart of the poet is whirl'd into folly and vice.
I would not marvel at either, but keep a temperate brain;
For not to desire or admire, if a man could learn it, were more
Than to walk all day like the sultan of old in a garden of spice.

VIII

For the drift of the Maker is dark, an Isis hid by the veil.
Who knows the ways of the world, how God will bring them
     about?
Our planet is one, the suns are many, the world is wide.
Shall I weep if a Poland fall? shall I shriek if a Hungary fail?
Or an infant civilization be ruled with rod or with knout?
I have not made the world, and He that made it will guide.

IX

Be mine a philosopher's life in the quiet woodland ways,
Where if I cannot be gay let a passionless peace be my lot,
Far-off from the clamour of liars belied in the hubbub of lies;
From the long-neck'd geese of the world that are ever hissing
     dispraise
Because their natures are little, and, whether he heed it or not,
Where each man walks with his head in a cloud of poisonous
     flies.

X

And most of all would I flee from the cruel madness of love,
The honey of poison-flowers and all the measureless ill.
Ah Maud, you milkwhite fawn, you are all unmeet for a wife.
Your mother is mute in her grave as her image in marble above;
Your father is ever in London, you wander about at your will;
You have but fed on the roses, and lain in the lilies of life.

135

XII

I

Birds in the high Hall-garden
    When twilight was falling,
Maud, Maud, Maud, Maud,
    They were crying and calling.

II

Where was Maud? in our wood;
    And I, who else, was with her,
Gathering woodland lilies,
    Myriads blow together.

III

Birds in our wood song
    Ringing through the valleys,
Maud is here, here, here,
    In among the lilies.

IV

I kiss'd her slender hand,
    She took the kiss sedately;
Maud is not seventeen,
    But she is tall and stately.

V

I to cry out on pride
    Who have won her favour!
Oh, Maud were sure of heaven
    If loveliness could save her.

VI

I know the way she went
    Home with her maiden's posy,
For her feet have touch'd the meadows,
    And left the daisies rosy.

VII

Birds in the high Hall-garden
    Were crying and calling to her,
Where is Maud, Maud, Maud?
    One is come to woo her.

VIII

Look, a horse at the door,
    And little King Charles is snarling,
Go back, my lord across the moor,
    You are not her darling.

ALFRED, LORD TENNYSON
1809–92

St Agnes' Eve

Deep on the convent-roof the snows
   Are sparkling to the moon:
My breath to heaven like vapour goes:
   May my soul follow soon!
The shadows of the convent-towers
   Slant down the snowy sward,
Still creeping with the creeping hours
   That lead me to my Lord:
Make thou my spirit pure and clear
   As are the frosty skies,
Or this first snowdrop of the year
   That in my bosom lies.

As these white robes are soiled and dark,
   To yonder shining ground:
As this pale taper's earthly spark,
   To yonder argent round;
So shows my soul before the Lamb,
   My spirit before Thee;
So in mine earthly house I am,
   To that I hope to be.
Break up the heavens, O Lord! and far,
   Thro' all yon starlight keen,
Draw me, Thy bride, a glittering star,
   In raiment white and clean.

He lifts me to the golden doors;
    The flashes come and go;
All heaven bursts her starry floors,
    And strows her lights below,
And deepens on and up! the gates
    Roll back, and far within
For me the Heavenly Bridegroom waits,
    To make me pure of sin.
The sabbaths of Eternity,
    One sabbath deep and wide –
A light upon the shining sea –
    The Bridegroom with his bride!

FRANCIS THOMPSON
1859–1907

Arab Love-Song

The hunchèd camels of the night
Trouble the bright
And silver waters of the moon.
The Maiden of the Morn will soon
Through Heaven stray and sing,
Star gathering.

Now while the dark about our loves is strewn,
Light of my dark, blood of my heart, O come!
And night will catch her breath up, and be dumb.

Leave thy father, leave thy mother
And thy brother;
Leave the black tents of thy tribe apart!
Am I not thy father and thy brother,
And thy mother?
And thou – what needest with thy tribe's black tents
Who hast the red pavilion of my heart?

KATHARINE TYNAN
1861–1931

The Choice

When skies are blue and days are bright
A kitchen-garden's my delight,
Set round with rows of decent box
And blowsy girls of hollyhocks.

Before the lark his Lauds hath done
And ere the corncrake's southward gone;
Before the thrush good-night hath said
And the young Summer's put to bed.

The currant-bushes' spicy smell,
Homely and honest, likes me well,
The while on strawberries I feast,
And raspberries the sun hath kissed.

Beans all a-blowing by a row
Of hives that great with honey go,
With mignonette and heaths to yield
The plundering bee his honey-field.

Sweet herbs in plenty, blue borage
And the delicious mint and sage,
Rosemary, marjoram, and rue,
And thyme to scent the winter through.

Here are small apples growing round,
And apricots all golden-gowned,
And plums that presently will flush
And show their bush a Burning Bush.

Cherries in nets against the wall,
Where Master Thrush his madrigal
Sings, and makes oath a churl is he
Who grudges cherries for a fee.

Lavender, sweet-briar, orris. Here
Shall Beauty make her pomander,
Her sweet-balls for to lay in clothes
That wrap her as the leaves the rose.

Take roses red and lilies white,
A kitchen garden's my delight;
Its gillyflowers and phlox and cloves,
And its tall cote of irised doves.

HENRY VAUGHAN
1621–95

Peace

I could not say that I have a favourite poem, because
poetry speaks to so many different moods, but if I had to
choose, this would be the one. I think the first two lines
are among the most beautiful in English poetry.

My soul, there is a country
   Far beyond the stars,
Where stands a wingèd sentry
   All skilful in the wars:
There above noise and danger
   Sweet Peace sits crowned with smiles,
And One born in a manger
   Commands the beauteous files.
He is thy gracious friend
   And – O my soul, awake! –
Did in pure love descend
   To die here for thy sake.
If thou canst get but thither,
   There grows the flower of Peace,
The Rose that cannot wither,
   Thy fortress, and thy ease.
Leave then thy foolish ranges
   For none can thee secure,
But one who never changes,
   Thy God, thy life, thy cure.

WALT WHITMAN

1819–92

O Captain! My Captain!

O Captain! my Captain! our fearful trip is done,
The ship has weather'd every rack, the prize we sought
    is won,
The port is near, the bells I hear, the people all exulting,
While follow eyes the steady keel, the vessel grim and daring;
       But O heart! heart! heart!
        O the bleeding drops of red!
          Where on the deck my Captain lies,
          Fallen cold and dead.

O Captain! my Captain! rise up and hear the bells;
Rise up – for you the flag is flung – for you the bugle trills,
For you bouquets and ribbon'd wreaths – for you the shores
    crowding,
For you they call, the swaying mass, their eager faces turning;
       Here, Captain! dear father!
        This arm beneath your head!
          It is some dream that on the deck
          You've fallen cold and dead.

My Captain does not answer, his lips are pale and still,
My father does not feel my arm, he has no pulse nor will;
The ship is anchor'd safe and sound, its voyage closed and
    done,
From fearful trip the victor ship comes in with object won;
       Exult, O shores! and sing, O bells!
        But I, with mournful tread,
          Walk the deck my Captain lies,
          Fallen cold and dead.

JOHN GREENLEAF WHITTIER
1807–92

Who fathoms the eternal thought?

Who fathoms the eternal thought?
　　Who talks of scheme and plan?
The Lord is God! He needeth not
　　The poor device of man.

Here in the maddening maze of things,
　　When tossed by storm and flood,
To one fixed ground my spirit clings:
　　I know that God is good.

I long for household voices gone,
　　For vanished smiles I long;
But God hath led my dear ones on,
　　And He can do no wrong.

I know not what the future hath
　　Of marvel or surprise,
Assured alone that life and death
　　His mercy underlies.

And if my heart and flesh are weak
　　To bear an untried pain,
The bruisèd reed He will not break,
　　But strengthen and sustain.

And so beside the silent sea
　　I wait the muffled oar;
No harm from Him can come to me
　　On ocean or on shore.

I know not where His islands lift
　　Their fronded palms in air;
I only know I cannot drift
　　Beyond His love and care.

JOHN GREENLEAF WHITTIER
1807–92

Dear Lord and Father of mankind

Dear Lord and Father of mankind,
  Forgive our feverish ways!
Reclothe us in our rightful mind;
In purer lives Thy service find,
  In deeper reverence, praise.

In simple trust like theirs who heard,
  Beside the Syrian sea,
The gracious calling of the Lord,
Let us, like them, without a word,
  Rise up and follow Thee.

O Sabbath rest by Galilee!
  O calm of hills above,
Where Jesus knelt to share with Thee
The silence of eternity,
  Interpreted by love!

With that deep hush subduing all
  Our words and works that drown
The tender whisper of Thy call,
As noiseless let Thy blessing fall
  As fell Thy manna down.

Drop Thy still dews of quietness,
  Till all our strivings cease;
Take from our souls the strain and stress,
And let our ordered lives confess
  The beauty of Thy peace.

146

Breathe through the pulses of desire
  Thy coolness and Thy balm;
Let sense be dumb, its heats expire:
Speak through the earthquake, wind, and fire,
  O still small Voice of calm!

CHARLES WILLIAMS
1886–1945

A Dream

No more in any house can I be at peace,
  Because of a house that waits, far off or near,
  To-morrow or (likelier) after many a year,
  Where a room and a door are that shall fulfil my fear.

For last night, dreaming, I stood in a house and saw
  Softly the room door open, and one came in,
  Its owner, and as round the edge his evil grin
  Peep'd ere he pass'd, I knew him for visible Sin.

Unwash'd, unshaven, frowsy, abominable,
  In a green greasy hat, a green greasy coat,
  Loose-mouth'd, with silent tread and the smell of the goat,
  He stole in, and helplessness stifled rage in my throat.

For this was he who came long since to my heart,
  This was he who enter'd the house of my soul long ago;
  Now he possesses imagination, and O
  I shall meet him yet in some brick-built house, I know.

He shall come, he shall turn from the long parch'd street he
    treads
  For ever, shuffling, hand rubb'd over hand unclean,
  Servile yet masterful, with satiate spleen
  Watching his houses, and muttering of things obscene.

He shall come to my flesh as he came last night to my dream;
  Eyes shall know him as soul and insight have known;
  Though all the world be there, I shall stand alone
  Watching him peer and enter and find out his own.

Noisier he shall not move, nor loudlier speak,
   Than the first sly motion of lewd delight in me
   Long since – which then I shall know none other than he
   Now visible, aged, and filled with monstrous glee.

Therefore now in terror I enter all houses, all rooms
   Enter in dread, and move among them in fear,
   Watching all doors, saying softly 'It draws more near
   Daily; and here shall it be in the end – or here?'

MARY WILSON
born 1916

I have indulged myself by including two of my own
poems. The first, 'St Cross', is part of a set of poems called
In Memoriam John Webster, and contains a reference to
Charles Williams, one of whose poems is in this book.

The second describes my grandchildren paddling in
the sea around the Isles of Scilly.

St Cross

In old St Cross, the blackbirds sing
All day among the cedar trees;
Wild briony and bindweed cling
Around the headstones, and a breeze
Is blowing through the waving grass,
And round the feet of ghosts, who pass

To wander up the curving Street,
Or drift unseen through College Halls,
Hoping some long-lost friend to meet
Among the portraits on the walls –
Until the booming of Great Tom
Summons both ghosts and students home.

Here, Town and Gown lie side by side;
And Maurice Bowra's simple stone
(And laurel wreath from Christmas-tide)
Are just six steps along the path
From where, in polished marble, lie
The station-master's family.

Charles Williams, poet, all alone
Beneath a drooping pure white rose,
'Under the Mercy', says his stone.
The keeper of this quiet plot
Has here, himself laid down to rest
Among the friends whom he loved best.

With downcast eyes, and folded hands
Near Walter Pater's plain stone cross
A terracotta angel stands.
For Kenneth Grahame, near the gate,
No willows weep, but blossom flies
Along the wind to where he lies.

Here are three brothers; crowned with fame
Were two of them – for Academe
Had paid its tribute to their name;
The middle brother, much beloved,
With falling leaves was swept away
In Isis, one October day.

A cry, a splash, an upturned boat –
An empty stream for those who ran
To see the rising bubbles float;
He was a Scholar, just eighteen.
The brothers mourned him through the years
And still remembered him with tears.

And as they sat secure in Hall,
Among the happy voices there
Did one young voice cry over all
'But what of me? What of my life?
Where are the honours for my brow?'
Three brothers rest together, now.

Soldiers and sailors, mountaineers,
Students from far across the world,
Doctors and nurses, engineers

Lie here with dons and scientists
And clergymen, both High and Low;
And over all, the grasses grow.

Sometimes I hear the organ play –
So sweet a sound, to pierce the heart
With echoes of another day;
Remember the Toccata, John,
Pealing in triumph through the night,
The chapel lit by candlelight?

And later, when the crowd had gone,
You played an evening hymn for me,
And in the quiet, still played on.
The shadows shook among the pews,
The candles guttered, one by one.
'Goodnight, dear friend, the concert's done.'

And now your grave is green with moss;
Yew-berries stain the Yorkshire stone
Which marks your place in old St Cross;
The meadow-grass is trodden down
By those who, all the summer through
Come here, to stand and think of you.

Yet clearly now, as one who sees
The image of a memory,
I see you limping through the trees,
Smiling, and shrugging-on your gown
And saying, just beyond full sight,
'Don't fret for me, for I'm *all right!*'

In old St Cross, all through the day,
The floating chimes of Merton clock
Signal the hours and years away;
And grief dulls to acceptance here –
How could I break the spell, and weep
Where Oxford's dreaming children sleep?

MARY WILSON

born 1916

Summer

Two little girls at the edge of the sea
Gaze at the water silently;
With ribbons of seaweed in each hand
They press their feet to the yielding sand.
Scarlet sail on a mizzen mast,
Oyster-catchers scurrying past,
Vapour trails in a brilliant sky,
Shag hanging out their wings to dry,
Fennel and mallow and bittersweet
Growing where pebbles and heather meet;
  This is a picture to hold in mind
  If winter is cold, and the world unkind,
  And summer is only a memory
  Of two little girls at the edge of the sea.

WILLIAM WORDSWORTH
1770–1850

The world is too much with us

The world is too much with us; late and soon,
Getting and spending, we lay waste our powers:
Little we see in Nature that is ours;
We have given our hearts away, a sordid boon!
This Sea that bares her bosom to the moon;
The winds that will be howling at all hours,
And are up-gathered now like sleeping flowers;
For this, for everything, we are out of tune;
It moves us not. – Great God! I'd rather be
A Pagan suckled in a creed outworn;
So might I, standing on this pleasant lea,
Have glimpses that would make me less forlorn;
Have sight of Proteus rising from the sea;
Or hear old Triton blow his wreathèd horn.

WILLIAM WORDSWORTH
1770–1850

From *Intimations of Immortality*

Our birth is but a sleep and a forgetting:
The Soul that rises with us, our life's Star,
      Hath had elsewhere its setting,
        And cometh from afar:
       Not in entire forgetfulness,
       And not in utter nakedness,
But trailing clouds of glory do we come
      From God, who is our home:
Heaven lies about us in our infancy!

Shades of the prison-house begin to close
      Upon the growing Boy,
But he beholds the light, and whence it flows,
      He sees it in his joy;
The Youth, who daily farther from the east
    Must travel, still is Nature's priest,
      And by the vision splendid
      Is on his way attended;
At length the Man perceives it die away,
And fade into the light of common day.

W. B. YEATS
1865–1939

In Memory of Eva Gore-Booth and Con Markiewicz

The light of evening, Lissadell,
Great windows open to the south,
Two girls in silk kimonos, both
Beautiful, one a gazelle.
But a raving autumn shears
Blossom from the summer's wreath;
The older is condemned to death,
Pardoned, drags out lonely years
Conspiring among the ignorant.
I know not what the younger dreams –
Some vague Utopia – and she seems,
When withered old and skeleton-gaunt,
An image of such politics.
Many a time I think to seek
One or the other out and speak
Of that old Georgian mansion, mix
Pictures of the mind, recall
That table and the talk of youth,
Two girls in silk kimonos, both
Beautiful, one a gazelle.

Dear shadows, now you know it all,
All the folly of a fight
With a common wrong or right.
The innocent and the beautiful
Have no enemy but time;
Arise and bid me strike a match
And strike another till time catch;
Should the conflagration climb,
Run till all the sages know.
We the great gazebo built,
They convicted us of guilt;
Bid me strike a match and blow.